Slaying the Marriage Dragons

A Biblical and Experiential Look at How to Deal with Issues in Marriage with Discussion Questions

RUSSELL J. LAMENDOLA

ISBN 978-1-63575-479-7 (Paperback)
ISBN 978-1-63575-480-3 (Digital)

Christian Faith Publishing, Inc.
296 Chestnut Street
Meadville, PA 16335
www.christianfaithpublishing.com

All Scripture is taken from the Ryrie NASB Study Bible. 1995, Moody Publishers, Chicago.

Printed in the United States of America

DEDICATION

To Misty: my wife, my cheerleader, my lover, my best friend, my helper, and the one who told me I could write this book. Without you, I would never have fully understood what love and marriage truly means. You are a gift from God, and I love you more each day.

As we have had to deal with marriage dragons in our life together, I thank you for being there through the mountains and valleys. It has been an honor to be your knight in shining armor to slay the marriage dragons with, and for, you. This truly has been an exciting and wonderful adventure together. I look forward to us continuing this journey together with God.

CONTENTS

Introduction...7

Chapter 1: Who Rules the Marriage Dragons? 11
Chapter 2: Recognizing Marriage Dragons..................16
Chapter 3: The Dragon of Communication..................20
Chapter 4: The Dragon of Sex 27
Chapter 5: The Dragon of Past Hurts 33
Chapter 6: The Dragon of Rejection............................40
Chapter 7: The Dragon of Uncertainty.......................48
Chapter 8: The Dragon of Lying..................................56
Chapter 9: The Dragon of Secrets................................61
Chapter 10: The Dragon of Unforgiveness.....................68
Chapter 11: The Dragon of Children 73
Chapter 12: The Dragon of the Umbilical Cord 83
Chapter 13: The Dragon of Money 90
Chapter 14: The Dragon of Anger 95
Chapter 15: The Dragon of Coveting 100
Chapter 16: The Dragon of Submission........................106
Chapter 17: The Dragon of Conflict 112
Chapter 18: The Dragon of Technology........................117
Chapter 19: The Dragon of Time 123
Chapter 20: The Dragon of Divorce 128
Chapter 21: Do Marriage Dragons Have Any Good in Them? ..135
Chapter 22: Conclusion..139

Epilogue: God's Desire for You Reading This Book 143

Introduction

"God created man in His own image, in the image of God He created him; male and female He created them. God blessed them; and God said to them, 'Be fruitful and multiply, and fill the earth, and subdue it; and rule over the fish of the sea and over the birds of the sky and over every living thing that moves on earth.'" (Genesis 1:27–28)

When one hears the word *marriage* today, many different thoughts may come to mind. Some may think they are not interested in spending a lifetime with one person, or they have been through painful breakups and are not interested in risking falling in love again. Others may have been through a horrific divorce and have decided they will never put themselves in a marriage covenant again. Still, others may consider themselves "stuck" in a lifeless, loveless marriage.

I have good news for any of you who may find yourselves in one of the categories above, or any other category: your marriage can be better than ever. You married the person you married because there was something about them that you fell in love with. That "something" is still there. It could be over time that a marriage dragon has crept in and affected parts of your marriage. If a dragon has shown himself, now is the time to slay it. It is never too late to save a struggling marriage.

Some of the topics and the biblical responses to these problems may be new to some of you, or you may not have thought that the Bible could give you specific answers to specific marital problems. I have great news for you: with Jesus Christ all things are possible, and you can have the marriage God designed for you to have. I pray that this book will help you no matter what your situation may be.

I have written this book from personal experience working with married couples for over a decade. I will also give you examples from my own marriage, and the solutions all come from biblical principles. I want you to know that you are not alone in a struggle you may be having.

There was one person who attended one of the marriage groups my wife and I were leading. It was her first time attending our group, and we had just met her. At the very end of the class, she commented to all of us, "I thought that I was the only person struggling with some of the issues we discussed today."

That is one of the weapons of the marriage dragons: to make you think that you are the only one having the problem and there is no help. I can tell you that this person is in a stronger marriage today.

In some cases, there may be more than one way to slay a dragon, but it all comes down to whether or not you are using biblical principles to find that solution. If you are, the problem will have a have a solution that will be from God Himself. It still may take some time to solve the problem, but if you bring God into it, the problem can, and will, be solved.

This is a book to help you gain some insight for your marriage. My hope is that you can use this book as a foundation to strengthen your marriage. I believe that single people can use this book to prepare themselves for marriage and for some of the issues they may come up against.

At the end of each chapter, there are a few questions to reflect on personally and to also discuss with your spouse. Please feel free to add your own questions that may pertain to the situation and circumstances in your marriage.

I need to add one more thing to this introduction: every person and every problem is different. This book is a general guide to give you some general strategies that you can use from the Bible and my personal experiences. These experiences come from my own marriage and from those marriages around me. If we do things God's way, we will be victorious.

You may not agree with everything I say in this book, but I would ask that you look at your marriage as God sees it. Read the scriptures that I include, and use them against the marriage dragon you are fighting. Please seek out other scriptures that relate to your dragon to defeat it.

I hope you enjoy reading this book. It has been an exciting journey writing it, and I pray that it helps protect your marriage against the dragons that are attempting to destroy it.

CHAPTER 1

Who Rules the Marriage Dragons?

"Be of sober spirit, be on the alert. Your adversary, the devil, prowls around like a roaring lion, seeking someone to devour." (1 Peter 5:8)

A dragon is a creature that sits silently in waiting. Most of the time, a dragon is not even noticed until it attacks. When a dragon is irritated and it begins its attack, not much can stand against it. By the time the dragon has attacked, it is usually too late, and the destruction has already occurred.

However, as with many stories where the dragon attacks, the townspeople find a way to defeat the dragon. The dragon either is killed or becomes a friend to the townspeople. Once the dragon is defeated or befriended, rebuilding of the town commences, and the townspeople go back to their lives.

Some of you are thinking to yourselves, "This is no fairy tale that I am in. My marriage is in serious trouble, and you are giving me Hollywood answers to a marital problem." No, I am giving you hope; just like the story where everyone comes together to defeat the dragon, so can you and your spouse do the same.

Every marriage dragon can be slain; you just have to work together to be successful. Marriage is, and always has been, one man and one woman coming together in one life. According to the Bible, you are one flesh, and you need to live as such. What happens to one happens to the other. Marriage is a team effort.

There are many marriage dragons that are waiting in hiding. Some of them are obvious and others not so much. I will take a look at some of these dragons and give you some biblical and basic answers to overcome the dragons that have appeared.

First, we need to look at Satan, who is the leader of the marriage dragons. It is his desire to defeat you and destroy the family unit today. Nothing pleases Satan more than when he can get a marriage on the rocks and then see it end in divorce. When a marriage ends in divorce, Satan laughs. It is time to stop his laughter, stop believing his lies, and get real with God about your marriage.

The Bible tells us in John 8:44 that "Satan is a murderer" and "the father of lies." Satan may be whispering in your ear right now that your marriage is so far gone that you will never recover from the issues you are having. He may be telling you that the pretty neighbor who has been showing you some attention is more caring than your wife will ever be. He might be telling you that the man at work who has shown you some compassion, and is listening to all your problems during the lunch break, is more loving than your husband will ever be.

Nothing could be further from the truth! The grass is not greener on the other side of the fence! One of my favorite sayings I use with married couples is, "If you want green grass, stay home and water your own lawn." The other side of the fence is very dangerous territory. Satan wants your marriage to fail, and he will do everything he can to make sure that happens.

You may be asking yourself, "Why would Satan lie to me?" The answer is simple: he lied to Jesus Christ thinking he actually had a chance to trick the Son of God into sinning. In Matthew 4:1–11 and Luke 4:1–13, Satan tests Jesus in three different ways. However, his primary goal was to make Jesus sin against God the Father and completely destroy the plan of redemption.

If Satan thinks he can trick the Son of God, do you really believe he would not try to lie to the sinners that we are as humans? If we are not grounded in the Word of God, it can be easy for us to fall into one of Satan's snares. We are fallen and sinful creations. We must be in God's Word to protect us before, and when, the dragons appear. Only then can we do spiritual battle. If we can recognize the dragons when they first appear, we will be ready to go to war as a couple and defeat the dragon that has shown up.

Ephesians 6:10–17 is one of the better-known scriptures of the Bible. It is the armor of God:

> *"Finally, be strong in the Lord and in the strength of His might. Put on your full armor of God, so that you will be able to stand firm against the schemes of the devil. For our struggle is not against flesh and blood, but against the rulers, against the powers, against the spiritual forces of wickedness in the heavenly places. Therefore, take up the full armor of God, so that you will be able to resist in the evil day, and having done everything, to stand firm. Stand firm therefore, having girded your loins with truth, and having put on the breastplate of righteousness, and having shod your feet with the preparation of the gospel of peace; in addition to all, taking up the shield of faith with which you*

will be able to extinguish all the flaming arrows of
the evil one. And take the helmet of salvation, and
the sword of the Spirit, which is the word of God."

Paul has much wisdom in all his writings, and this is no exception. Paul lays out the way that the Christian needs to go into battle on a daily basis. Paul warns of the evil one and his schemes and flaming arrows. If the Christian is constantly moving toward Jesus Christ, the arrows have less of a chance to hit them. A moving target is always harder to hit! Be prepared daily to be in battle with the devil and his dragons he is unleashing into your marriage.

Scripture is vital when heading into battle with a dragon. The verse in 2 Timothy 3:16 says, "All Scripture is inspired by God and profitable for teaching, for reproof, for correction, for training in righteousness; so that the man of God may be adequate, equipped for every good work."

Are you equipped for every good work? Are you willing to be trained in righteousness? My prayer is that I hope you are. If you are, please keep reading this book, and be ready to enter into battle and slay your marriage dragons!

Discussion Questions for the Ruler of the Marriage Dragons

1. Who releases the marriage dragons?
2. What do you think you can you do as a couple to slay your marriage dragons?
3. What lies have you been listening to that may be endangering your marriage and feeding a marriage dragon?
4. Are you willing to put on your armor and go into battle to slay your dragons as a couple?

5.   What scriptures can the two of you use to defeat the ruler of the marriage dragons?

Notes

CHAPTER 2

Recognizing Marriage Dragons

*"But the Lord is faithful, and He will protect you
from the evil one." (2 Thessalonians 3:3)*

God created all of us differently. If we were to sit down together at
a shopping mall and observe people, we would see, and hear, the
differences in every person walking by. There would be differences
in height, hair, eyes, voice tones, and all the other differences we are
familiar with.

The one difference we cannot see is how they differ in handling
issues. We also cannot see what these people have been through in
their lives. We would not be able to see the joys, hurts, victories, or
defeats they have experienced.

We would see people smile, which usually means that they are
happy. We might also see people cry, which usually means sadness.
However, it is the emotions deep down that cannot be seen. These
are the dragons that people may be hiding deep down inside, and
these can be the dragons that are looking for a way out.

Everyone handles problems in their own way. It could be that they have had a very difficult childhood and they only know some type of pain and frustration in their lives. They may have suffered a great loss in their lives and are still grieving it. None of us truly knows what another has been through. We may have experienced the same type of situation, but the emotions that one person has, another person cannot fully comprehend.

This is especially true in the marriage covenant. When God brings two people together in marriage, He is bringing together two imperfect people with some type of history. Some of this history—or baggage, as it is called—will be carried from the husband's or wife's childhood and directly into the marriage. This is where the problems may arise.

Some of the ways that marriage dragons can be recognized are through behaviors. Let's look at the infamous toothpaste tube. One of the comments I have heard over and over again is that one of the partners squeezes the toothpaste tube from the middle while the other squeezes it from the end.

Seems like a situation that does not cause any problems, until it happens and one spouse remembers that one of their parents would become angry when the tube was squeezed in a way the parent did not want it to be. As soon as this memory, of how one of the parents reacted when this squeezing of the toothpaste tube occurred, this dragon shows up. The spouse gets angry and starts yelling about the tube being squeezed in some horrific way. It is not the squeezing that is causing the problem; it is the *memory* of the squeezing that is causing the problem.

I actually know of a woman who told me that she had divorced a man over the way the toothpaste tube was handled. It took a while, but after some conversation with her, I realized it had nothing to do with the tube: it had to do with a memory that was from her early life. This marriage lasted less than a year. Instead of facing the issue head-on, she decided to run.

It is strange that for the years after this failed marriage, this person could not continue on with any relationship for very long. She could not commit to anyone. To this day, she is still alone looking for the perfect man to come along. Just so you know, this marriage failed back in the eighties. So for over thirty years, she has been carrying around a memory that has gotten in the way of every relationship she has ever tried to have.

Another way that dragons can be recognized is through words. If communication is present in a marriage, which it should be, the dragons should be quite easy to deal with. I will be addressing communication in detail in the next chapter, but this needs to be looked at here first.

When words are spoken, they cannot be taken back. When something is said, and it reminds one of the spouses about a painful time in their life, they may lash out at their spouse because it brings up a memory. When a particular word, or words, is spoken, it can trigger a reaction that may not be expected. This will leave one of the spouses in a state of bewilderment trying to figure out how an innocent comment could be such a problem.

Dragons do not always work alone. Sometimes they bring other types of dragons with them. When hordes of dragons show up, it compounds the issues and problems. It is important to understand how each dragon works so when they do appear, either alone or with another, you can recognize them and go into battle to defeat the dragon.

As you read through this book, be aware of all their tactics so you are not blindsided by any of them.

Dragons can be hiding deep in a person's heart. When a dragon is provoked, it will come screaming out of its hiding place and cause extreme damage. There is good news, and that news is that if the dragon is faced together, the marriage can be saved, and can grow, from the dragon attack. Once the dragon is defeated, it can be used to strengthen a marriage, and this will glorify God in the process.

Discussion Questions for Recognizing Marriage Dragons

1. What kind of baggage do you have that may awaken a marriage dragon?
2. Are you willing to discuss the dragon(s) that you have recognized with your spouse?
3. Is there a "toothpaste tube" in your marriage? What are your plans to deal with this particular dragon?
4. If there is a marriage dragon in your life, did he bring along another with him that you may not have initially recognized?

Notes

CHAPTER 3

The Dragon of Communication

"But no human being can tame the tongue. It is a restless evil, full of deadly poison." (James 3:8)

Be careful what you say, or the Dragon of Communication will come out of its lair and cause serious damage. This damage can be devastating if it is allowed to run amok in the home. Imagine a fire-breathing dragon let loose in your home. The damage can be costly and takes years to repair, if repairs can be made at all.

Being able to communicate is something that many people may not know how to do. Communication is more than verbal. It can be a look, a physical movement, or silence. Any of these types of communication will send a different message. What person has not received the "look" from someone? Actions can be very powerful and very communicative.

Words, of course, can still be the most powerful way to get a situation handled or to start a situation. Ask any man who has been asked this question: "Do I look good in this outfit?" At the moment that question is asked, the man has much to consider:

"Should I tell the truth even if it does hurt?"

"Should I lie?"

"How do I get out of the house without answering this question?"

"What if I just smile and hug her, will that get me out of this mess?"

I have bad news, men: she is looking for an answer, and if your marriage is based on truth, which it should be, this question can be answered lovingly and without fear of sleeping on the couch the rest of your life.

First, this is an unfair question to ask. Ladies, please do not ever ask this question, unless you are really ready to hear the answer. I know men who are brutally honest and they are not afraid to answer honestly. Let's face it, we are all getting older, and our bodies have a tendency to "change" in all kinds of ways. Most of these ways are not pleasant. It is what it is.

However, when communicating the answer to this question, if it is asked, a husband only needs to say that their wife is beautiful in anything they wear. This is not a lie, because our wives *are* beautiful no matter what they wear. They are made in the image of God, and that makes them beautiful. I would hope that all of you men who are reading this book find your wife beautiful and you tell her that.

This may not be the best example of how communication can cause some problems in a marriage, but it occurs more often than one thinks. The dragon that can be released by a word that does not edify can be dangerous. Proverbs 18:21 says, "Death and life are in the power of the tongue, and those that love it will eat its fruit."

One harsh word today could last for many tomorrows. Proverbs 15:1 says, "A gentle answer turns away wrath, but a harsh word stirs up anger." Are you using your words to calm a situation, or do you keep talking and continue in making a situation worse? Each of us is responsible for our words; we must use them for edification and not to tear someone, especially our spouses, apart.

A big part of communicating is listening. Communication is a two-way street. One person talks, the other listens. If one is always speaking and not giving their spouse the opportunity to speak, this is not communicating. In James 1:19, it says, "This you know, my beloved brethren. But everyone must be quick to hear, slow to speak and slow to anger." Notice that James is telling the reader that we must be ready to hear, think before speaking, and not let what is being said anger us.

Proverbs 18:13 says, "He who gives an answer before he hears, It is folly and shame to him." Not only do we need to listen, but also we need to hear what our spouse is saying. There is a difference between hearing and listening. When you hear something, you can act on it. I can listen to things all day long, but until I hear what my wife is saying, there can be no real action or change.

If a spouse has problems with talking and is not hearing, there is a method that I have seen work numerous times. I call it the "I have something in my hand, and I will talk only when I am holding this object" method. To perform this method, one spouse holds a small object in their hand. You can use any item that is small enough to hold.

There is a given amount of time that is decided on for the first spouse to speak. When the spouse is holding this object, they are to do all the talking. When the spouse who is talking is finished speaking, they take the object and give it to their spouse; this means it is that spouse's turn to talk.

If you are not holding the object, you are to be quiet. It is important to focus on your spouse and not only listen but also hear what your spouse is saying. Questions can be asked when it is your turn to speak, and the answers should be given at that time. Only the answer to the asked question should be given.

This works better than you may think, but it may take practice. I was a person who would only hear parts of what my wife was saying. I was one who was thinking why she was talking. I was always preparing my "rebuttal" for anything she was saying. My motto was "My thoughts are important too!"

That may be true, but Misty needed to have a husband who listened to her wants, needs, desires, and concerns. She did not need a husband who was always trying to fix a problem or hear only parts of what she was saying. She deserved more than that, and so does your spouse.

While we are on the subject of fixing things, it helps for us to know men are fixers by nature. I know some men who break things more than fix them, but we need to listen to our wives first. Many times, they just want to share how their day went and their concerns with us, not have us fix everything they are discussing.

One of the ways I have worked through this type of situation is that I ask Misty if she wants me to fix anything or just listen to what she is saying. Once I know if she needs something fixed or not, then I can move forward with fixing or I can just sit and listen.

Men, one more thing: it is possible to sit and listen to your wife. It is very frustrating to me to hear men say that they do not "have time" to listen to their wives. Yes, you do. You *make* this time to communicate.

One of the most destructive forms of communication is one that you do not have with your spouse. It is the communication of speaking poorly *about* your spouse with your friends or family. There is nothing more devastating than when you get with your friends and begin to tell them how awful your spouse is.

Once you start this type of communicating, the Dragon of Communication goes into full attack mode. When someone else hears this type of talk, they jump right into the conversation and agree with everything you say. When this "group mentality" starts, the words that are spoken could last for years.

Eventually, whatever you are complaining about to your friends will be corrected, but the ideas that your friends now have about your spouse will change relationships. They will look at your spouse differently because of what you have spoken.

My suggestion is that if you are angry with your spouse you tell them about your hurt and anger and stay away from verbally destroying them to others. How would you feel if it was you on the receiving end of this attack? I have seen this done in some of the groups that my wife and I have led in the past, and you can see the pain on the spouse's face that comes from being humiliated in front of the group when the words are spoken.

Once these words come out, they are impossible to get back. They have already done the damage. I imagine the conversation that these people have on the ride home would be interesting at best. Never, ever say anything demeaning about your spouse in public or with your friends and family.

The final type of communication that I would like to discuss is, to me, the most important one. This communication is prayer. I cannot emphasize how important prayer is to the married couple. It should be done on a daily basis, and this time of prayer is a time of intimacy that cannot, and should not, be ignored. When a couple prays together, they bring God into their marriage in a special and unique way.

When Misty prays out loud, I find that she is more sensitive to the Holy Spirit and she may pray about things that I do not know about yet. The same goes for me, as I pray the Holy Spirit may stir something in me to pray about that Misty does not know about. These times of prayer are some of the most intimate times I have ever had with Misty; however, it has not always been this way.

I am going to say something now that most men will question: praying together can be more intimate than sex. If you do not believe me, try it. Praying together also increases the intimacy when sex does occur.

When Misty and I got married, she asked me to pray with her every day. She had not been a Christian as long as I had been, and I was not willing to pray with her. I believed prayer was very personal, which it is, but she wanted that closeness that prayer brings.

Her requests for us to pray together went on for days, weeks, and months. I was not listening, or hearing, what she was asking. I thought I knew better because I had been a Christian longer than she had been. What I failed to understand was that she wanted a closeness that only prayer could provide.

Then one day, she finally got tired of asking and stopped her requests, at least for a while. When she started again, she asked just a few times before her frustration reached a fever pitch. When I said no to her final request to pray with her, she looked me in the face and said this: "If you don't want to pray with me, that's fine. Jesus will be the husband that you don't want to be." And she walked away.

I can tell you that in that moment in time, conviction came upon me, and my heart broke. This conviction came not only because I had let Misty down but also because I had failed God as a husband and as a spiritual leader of my home. I immediately asked God for forgiveness and then Misty.

I can tell you that in over sixteen years of marriage, we have only missed a couple of nights of prayer. Those missed nights of prayer were because one of us had surgery, or if one us was ill and we were not coherent enough to pray. I can also tell you that this time of daily prayer has changed, and saved, our marriage. In those times of trials, when the enemy attacks your marriage, praying together will be the only thing you may have to hold on to.

In the decade that I have led a marriage group, I will tell you the one thing that almost every single wife has told me is that she wishes her husband would pray with her. When the husband starts to pray with his wife, things change for the better. When you bring God into your marriage that way, there is no other thing that can happen. You will be closer to your spouse than you can ever imagine.

I would challenge you to start this prayer time today. Do not wait. It may be a little uncomfortable to start with, but I can guarantee that in a few days it will be so comfortable that you will wonder how you have not done this before. It will be so natural, and you will miss the time of prayer if you do not have it.

So do you want to change your marriage and defeat the dragons together? Then let me offer you this unsolicited advice: men, take your wife by the hand and pray with her. Make time each day to become intimate in prayer with God and your wife. I promise you that it will strengthen your marriage and you will become closer than you ever thought possible.

Discussion Questions for the Dragon of Communication

1. How is communication in your marriage?
2. How can communication be improved in your marriage?
3. Ladies, do you give your husband the "look" when his back is turned or to his face?
4. Men, are you listening, or are in a hurry to fix something, as your wife speaks to you?
5. What Scripture/biblical story do you think of when you hear the word *communication*?
6. Are you praying together as husband and wife each and every day?
7. What scriptures can the two of you use to defeat a Dragon of Communication?

Notes

CHAPTER 4

The Dragon of Sex

*"Stop depriving one another, except by agreement
for a time, so that you may devote yourselves to
prayer, and come together again so that Satan will
not tempt you because of your lack of self-control."
(1 Corinthians 7:5)*

Sex. The word can bring up a lot of thoughts and emotions. It is a topic that is seldom talked about in Christian circles. Yet God is very clear in Scripture that it is something that has a rightful place in our marriages, and God has given us this great gift of physical closeness.

The question is this: "If sex is good for married couples, how can it be a dragon?" Great question! We need to understand why God created sex to begin with. Let's go back to Genesis for this one. Genesis 1:28 says, "God blessed them; and God said to them, 'Be fruitful and multiply, and fill the earth, and subdue it; and rule over the fish of the sea and over the birds of the sky and over every living thing that moves on the earth.'" God designed sex so that man and woman could reproduce and have children to "fill the earth."

Some of you reading this book may be having some problems conceiving a child. My wife and I have never been able to conceive due to some physical problems that she had. It took nothing away from our marriage. When sin entered the world, our bodies were cursed with sin, and that sometimes includes physical problems and illness. This was just the way it happened to manifest itself in our lives. God knew our struggle to conceive, and it did not stop us from rejoicing with others who were able to conceive.

Another reason that God created sex was for pleasure and intimacy. In the next chapter, Genesis 2:24, it says, "For this reason a man shall leave his father and his mother, and be joined to his wife; and they shall become one flesh." This marriage union is to have a physical component to it, and it is meant to be permanent union between a man and a woman.

It is important to understand that some of you who are reading this may have some physical challenges, and the physical part of your marriage may be a struggle for you. Please understand that God knows your concerns and problems. Love exceeds the physical aspect of any marriage relationship. Intimacy can still be a part of your marriage, just in a different way. Never think that because there may be a challenge in this area of your life that God has forgotten you. He has not, and He will not.

So far, it sounds like sex is a good thing and not a dragon. However, this can change quickly in a marriage, and the married couple needs to be on high alert. As we are physical created beings, we are designed to share our bodies with our spouses. Paul addresses this in 1 Corinthians 7:4: "The wife does not have authority over her own body, but the husband does; and likewise also the husband does not have authority over his own body, but the wife does." Paul is just reiterating that we are one flesh.

The Dragon of Sex can show up when one of the spouses does not keep the marital bed pure. This does not have to be a physical event. It can be an emotional affair, where a spouse finds himself or herself thinking about someone else. Eventually, thoughts can turn into actions, and this is where the problems of the Dragon of Sex arise. If one of the spouses has begun an emotional affair, the mind has already started to think about a physical affair. Not to say that this will happen, but the scenario has begun that needs to be stopped before sin occurs within the marriage.

Matthew 5:28 says, "But I say to you that everyone who looks at a woman with lust for her has already committed adultery with her in his heart." How are you looking at that other person? This passage is for wives too. Ladies, by application, you need to be careful how you look at others. In a day where there are romance novels, soap operas, and many other types of media that have a twisted view of romance, more women are getting involved in worldly thoughts that they should not be having.

This dragon can also show up if one spouse wants to have sex more, or maybe another spouse wants to have sex less. This can be a serious issue if not discussed. There may be a physical or emotional issue that is taking place. If so, a professional should be contacted to see what the problem might be.

Sex can also be used as a weapon. Ladies, you will not like me saying this, but most of the time, it is you who will withhold sex from your husbands because you are angry or you are trying to get something from him. This is an extremely dangerous thing to do. The verse in 1 Corinthians 7:4 does address this situation: you both give to each other. Now it must be understood that illness or some type of physical injury can cause some exception. You need to be loving and not force yourself on a sick, or injured, spouse.

Men, do not throw this Scripture out at your wife after a long day. If you do, you can release the Dragon of Sex. Women who are stay-at-home moms work hard—very hard. Put a job on top of that, and they are putting in long hours. Do not come home all dirty and smelly after a long day and want to be romantic. That will lead to one of those looks that no man wants, and a look you probably deserve.

Another Dragon of Sex can be the Dragon of Premarital Sex. I cannot tell you how many times I have heard Christians tell me that premarital sex is fine. Jesus has a different view. In Mark 7:20–22, one of the first words He uses to describe evil is "fornications." This word is used to describe all sexual immorality, including sex outside of marriage.

In 1 Corinthians 6:9–10, Paul explains what Jesus is saying this way: "Or do you not know that the unrighteous will not inherit the kingdom of God? Do not be deceived; neither fornicators, nor idolaters, nor adulterers, nor effeminate, nor homosexuals, nor thieves, nor the covetous, nor drunkards, nor revilers, nor swindlers, will inherit the kingdom of God."

The first sin that Paul states is "fornicators." Please understand that this sin is no worse that any other sin, but it is different as it affects the physical body. The verse in 1 Corinthians 6:18–19 says, "Flee immorality. Every other sin that a man commits is outside the body, but the immoral man sins against his own body. Or do you not know that your body is a temple of the Holy Spirit who is in you, whom you have from God, and that you are not your own?"

Paul is simply stating that any sexual sin committed will have some effect on the spiritual body, along with the physical problems that could also occur.

Hebrews 13:4 says, "Marriage is to be held in honor among all, and the marriage bed is to be undefiled; for fornicators and adulterers God will judge." The Dragon of Adultery is a big one. It is one that is birthed from the Dragon of Sex. I pray that it is a dragon that anyone reading this book will never have to deal with.

The reasons for one person having an adulterous affair are many, but I can tell you that communication is key. If you are struggling in your marriage and are considering going outside of the marriage, you must be willing to discuss these emotions with your spouse. You must also be open if your spouse comes to you struggling with the temptation of a sexual sin.

In either case, it must be discussed with love and understanding. You may not feel like loving your spouse if they come to you and want to tell you about the emotions they may be feeling toward another, but love is always the key.

You may be wondering how a marriage can continue after one spouse commits adultery. The answer is simple to say, not always simple to do, and that word is *forgiveness*. How do you forgive another who has betrayed you so deeply? Again, this will take work. This may include biblical counseling, accountability partners, and a whole lot of patience. However, through the power of forgiveness and some work, the marriage can go on. In some cases, the marriage can become stronger, but both parties must be willing to work hard together.

The Dragon of Sex includes pornography. I am not going to go into all the details of what pornography can do to a human mind, but I will tell you that pornography is dangerous, very dangerous, and there is never a time where people should be watching this twisted view of sex. The leader of the marriage dragons will tell you that it is fine to watch this with your spouse, but I can tell you that is it not. You are allowing something into your home and mind that should not be there.

Do not ever use pornography to bring more "excitement" into your marriage. It will destroy your marriage by attacking the sexual-intimacy part of your marriage. If you are watching pornography by yourself looking for "pointers," I can tell you that this is just one more lie from Satan. It would be impossible for any of us to be able to "perform" like the people do in these films, and you will do nothing but compare your spouse to what you have seen. Simply put, stay away from this garbage.

In closing this chapter, I must give one other warning: flirting is dangerous. I have already discussed emotional affairs and how they can be damaging. Flirting is where this can start. If you are saying or doing anything around a member of the opposite sex that you would not say, or do, with your spouse, you are asking for this dragon to show up.

Everything starts with a thought, and thoughts can lead to actions. I have seen this type of dragon show up quickly, and they usually sneak up on people. The Dragon of Sex is a sly and cunning dragon. He is also one of the most dangerous. Be careful how you act and what you say around the opposite sex.

Discussion Questions for the Dragon of Sex

1. Why did God design sex?
2. Can you speak with your spouse about your sexual desires without fear?
3. How is the sin of adultery different than other sins?
4. Is there a relationship that you may be developing outside of the marriage covenant that you should probably not be?
5. How is an emotional affair dangerous?
6. Have you flirted with a member of the opposite sex recently?
7. Have you or your spouse seen any pornography lately? If it is in your home, are you willing to remove it from your house to kill this dragon?
8. What scriptures can the two of you use to defeat a Dragon of Sex?

Notes

CHAPTER 5

The Dragon of Past Hurts

"Brethren, I do not regard myself as having laid hold of it yet; but one thing I do: forgetting what lies behind and reaching forward to what lies ahead, I press on toward the goal for the prize of the upward call of God in Christ Jesus." (Philippians 3:13–14)

The past. We all have one. Some parts of our past are wonderful, and other parts are painful. The one thing that we all do with our past is to bring those experiences into our present. It is important to know that we must be cautious with our memories and how they can affect our present relationships.

When the Dragon of Past Hurts rears its ugly head, circumstances can turn disastrous quickly. All it may take for this dragon to show up is a word, a look, or possibly something as simple as a song that reminds someone of a bad experience. If you find that a bad memory comes flooding back, know it must be dealt with quickly.

These past hurts can be anything from being fired from a job, parents who were nonsupportive, churches that have caused hurt, past relationships that ended poorly, or a host of other reasons. It is important to remember that we are created with emotions and memories, and these can work together to help us grow or tear us down. It is our responsibility to make sure that our past hurts stay in the past and that we do not bring them into any present relationship, including our marriages.

Sharing our past hurts with our spouse is important. Once a spouse knows what hurts we have experienced, they are in a better position to help. This is why it is important to have open communication in the marriage. One should always feel safe in the marriage, and this safety is important for all communication. By discussing past hurts, one spouse will be able to understand why their spouse may struggle when this dragon shows up.

One of the reasons we get married is to share our lives with another whom God has brought into our lives. At any given moment in time, we are in the present. As you are reading these words, you are "presently" doing so. Hopefully, you will continue to read through this book, and by doing so, you are looking ahead to what is coming in the next chapter.

Our lives are the same. We are constantly moving forward to the next chapter. Only by leaving the past "chapter" behind will we be able to move forward. If we are to stay in one chapter, we will not gain any understanding of what will occur next. The same is true for our marriages and other relationships. Just because you were hurt in the past does not mean that the present relationship will hurt you.

Depending on one's personality will depend on how easy these past hurts will be to overcome. As we are all created differently, the way we handle hurts will be different also. This is why we need to be patient with our spouses if they are struggling with a Dragon of a Past Hurt. The verse in 1 Corinthians 16:14 says, "Let all that you do be done in love." This includes helping your spouse go through a struggle with a past hurt. We must show tenderness, patience, and love to show support to our spouse.

There may be a time when there needs to be a professional counselor involved when dealing with certain hurts. If so, you must still be patient as they go through the process. Some of these hurts may be so deep that a professional counselor is the only way to help your spouse. There is nothing wrong with seeking help. I must give a warning here: if the hurt is deep and your spouse needs a professional to help them, please do not try to help them yourself. An unqualified person can do more damage if they try to help. Please be careful.

If a Dragon of Past Hurts shows up, it is up to the married couple to discuss it and then conquer it. There should not be any condemnation for the spouse who is struggling. The worst thing that can be done is for one spouse to tell the other, "Just get over it already, it was in your past!" This will only feed the dragon and anger it. The objective would be to contain the dragon and get rid of it as quickly as possible.

This type of dragon can be one of the most dangerous. When one spouse starts looking at the other spouse through the eyes of their past and they start comparing that person to someone whom they knew in their past, they are asking for trouble.

Every person in this world is different. Comparing one person to another is detrimental and dangerous. This is especially true if there was a long-term relationship with another person whom you keep comparing your spouse to. If you keep looking for your spouse to hurt you, as someone else might have, you will probably get what you are looking for.

One of the sayings I use when guiding people is, "If you look for something hard enough, you will find it." This is especially true if you have been hurt in the past. Please find a way to move on away from the hurt. Why would you want to hold on to a hurt that someone brought to you years ago?

My unsolicited advice to you would be to not give them one more second of your life. Every moment you spend looking back and holding on to those past hurts gives that person, or persons, more of a hold on your life. It's time to stop allowing them any more access to your life. Find a way to forgive them and free yourself so you can move on to a healthy, happy marriage.

Forgiving and moving on is probably one of the most difficult things one can do. Making the decision to forgive and forget is easy; it's the actually forgiving and forgetting that can be a problem. You are not alone in your struggle. By nature, we all want justice, and we are all capable of thinking up some pretty wild ways to get revenge on others who have hurt us.

I can tell you that God has it all in His hands. Romans 12:19 says, "Never take your own revenge, beloved, but leave room for the wrath of God, for it is written, 'Vengeance is mine, I will repay', says the Lord." I do not know about you, but I can say for myself that if God is going to bring justice to a situation, that is good enough for me. He may not bring the justice that is desired right away. He may wait days, weeks, months, or years, but He will bring justice to His children. He is a just God, and He loves to right the wrongs done to his children.

In Leviticus 19:18, it says, "You shall not take vengeance, nor bear any grudge against the sons of your people, but you shall love your neighbor as yourself; I am the Lord." Both of these scriptures tell me that God knows and understands our hurts and those who have hurt us. These scriptures also tell me that He has this all under control.

We must also be careful with what we expect from God in these situations. We should never look for God to "strike down" those who have hurt us. Scripture clearly states that we should pray for them. Jesus makes it clear in Matthew 5:43–45 how we should handle those who have hurt us:

"You have heard that it was said, 'You shall love your neighbor and hate your enemy.' "But I say to you, love your enemies and pray for those who persecute you, so that you may be sons of your Father who is in heaven; for He causes His sun to rise on the evil and the good, and sends rain on the righteous and the unrighteous."

Allow God to handle your enemies for you, and when you pray for those who have hurt you, your heart will soften toward them. God may answer your prayers for them and bring that person to a relationship with Jesus Christ.

If your spouse has hurt you during your marriage and then they hurt you again in the same way, what do you do? You need to forgive them again. All of us have some habitual sin in our life that we may be struggling with, and it is important to know that the person whom we married has the same struggle.

If they have hurt you and you have forgiven and then they do the exact same thing, you need forgive them again. The hurt may be deeper the second time, or third, but forgiveness still needs to be granted. You may have to deal with the emotions of the hurt, and that may take a little time. Be patient.

If your spouse hurts you and forgiveness is not granted, the Dragon of Past Hurts will come screaming out of its lair and start attacking. It looks for those who have been hurt in their marriage, and can use this hurt to continue the lack of trust and unforgiveness to keep the hurt alive.

One important thing to remember is that every one of us is responsible for our emotions and how we handle them. There is nothing wrong with hurting, it happens to all of us. The problem comes when we refuse to let go of the pain and hold on to it longer than we need to. When we get hurt, we should always come out of the pain learning some lesson.

Some things I say are the following: "Pain is the precursor to change" and "The lessons we learn in life are usually the ones that hurt the most." Embrace your pain, learn from it, and then let it go. This is especially true in our marriages. We should never punish our husbands or wives for a struggle they may be experiencing.

What if the hurt was from a fellow brother or sister in Christ? I have to go back to the words of Jesus Christ in Matthew 18:21–22 : "Then Peter came and said to Him, 'Lord, how often shall my brother sin against me and I forgive him? Up to seven times?' Jesus said to him, 'I do not say to you, up to seven times, but up to seventy times seven.'"

It may be hard to forgive, but Jesus tells us it is possible. Truth be told, it can be harder to forgive a brother or sister in Christ as most of us expect fellow Christians to act in a certain way. That way should be with love and grace. However, we are all sinners, and sometimes, our brothers and sisters in Christ bring us pain. I would be willing to guess that those of you reading this book have hurt someone else too. We should show the same grace to them that we would want them to show to us.

In a marriage, we may compare our spouse to the one who has hurt us, but when that Dragon of Past Hurt shows up, we need to defeat it quickly by talking to our spouse and explaining what the past hurt was and how it is affecting the marriage in the present. This dragon may also appear when our spouses hurt us. It does not matter how deep the hurt is; it can be dealt with, and your marriage can be better than ever.

Discussion Questions for the Dragon of Past Hurts

1. Are you dealing with any past hurts?
2. Can you speak with your spouse about your past hurts? If not, why not?
3. If your spouse has hurt you, are you holding that hurt over them?
4. Has your spouse said or done something that has awakened a Dragon of Past Hurts in your life?
5. How can you deal with a Dragon of Past Hurts?
6. What scriptures can the two of you use to defeat a Dragon of Past Hurts?

Notes

CHAPTER 6

The Dragon of Rejection

"If the world hates you, you know that it has hated Me before it hated you." (John 15:18)

Every once in a while, a rare event occurs with a marriage dragon. Instead of bringing along another marriage dragon, a dragon will birth another dragon to cause issues in a marriage.

The Dragon of Rejection is one of these dragons. It is directly related to the Dragon of Past Hurts, but it stands alone because of the damage that it can cause.

Looking at the Scripture that opens this chapter, one can see that Jesus knew rejection all too well. There are many others from the Bible who have felt the sting of rejection also. Moses, Joseph, and Paul come immediately to mind. What I am saying is that if you have been rejected—and most of us have at one time or another—know you are in very good company.

Some of you may say to yourself that the rejection you have first felt so long ago is still with you today. I am not surprised, as rejection is one of the hurts that is very difficult to come to terms with. The pain of rejection is far-reaching and can be long-lasting.

The Dragon of Rejection is one of the most dangerous of all the dragons because it is so personal. When most marriage dragons attack, they go after both of you. When the Dragon of Rejection attacks, it attacks one of you personally and wants you to think that you are alone in your pain. Here is where this dragon excels. It wants you to think that no one cares about you and you are the only one who has ever been rejected.

Here is the truth: even if everyone on this planet rejected you, God would still hold His arms open to hold you. When someone is rejected, it cuts to the heart of the person and sits in the deepest part of the heart until it is dealt with. It is also one of the most difficult of all dragons to defeat. This is one of the most painful dragon attacks to experience.

The thought of being rejected in a marriage can be paralyzing, especially if there is a rejection memory that you may be holding on to. It is very important to talk with your spouse and let them know that a Dragon of Rejection is with you. This will become important because if your husband or wife is to say something to you that awakens this dragon, you may not be able to restrain the hurt it brings. Memories can be both good and bad.

Unfortunately, if this dragon starts to attack, it will not be pleasant. The memories of a rejection can quickly return and overpower you. If this happens, the first thing you may do is lash out at the one who has reminded you of this pain.

This is why it is never a good idea to leave when you are having a discussion or argument. Getting in your car and driving off is the ultimate rejection. If you do this, you are telling your spouse that they are not worth sticking around for and you are not willing to respect them enough to talk to them. This can be devastating. I cannot emphasize this enough: never leave. Stay and work through the difficulties.

Dealing with this dragon is extremely difficult, especially if it has followed you for a while. First, it is important to understand how this dragon can be released. It is based on senses. This dragon works through all five senses. Sight, sound, touch, smell, or taste can all release the Dragon of Rejection. If your spouse has "activated" one of your senses that has brought you back to a time of rejection, it is important to do everything possible to keep your emotions in check.

It will not be as easy as it sounds. It is possible your spouse who has released this dragon was the one who may have rejected you before. It is also likely that it was not your spouse who was the one who had rejected you but someone else in your past. If it was your spouse, then you must speak with them about how their words, actions, or some other form of communication has touched one of your senses in a negative way. If you immediately go on the defensive, you will start something that may take some time to recover from. Do not punish the innocent for something that had happened to you in your past from another person.

The best way to deal with this dragon is to make sure you know what event has been triggered. The odds are that you have been rejected more than once in your lifetime, and it helps greatly to know which specific rejection you are dealing with. You just need to sit down and figure out why this is so painful, and then you can move forward with the healing process.

Healing can be difficult, and it may take a professional to guide you through the process, but it is possible to handle this dragon with God and your spouse. First, communication is key. You need to be honest with God, your spouse, and yourself. If you are hurting from a past rejection, admit to God that you are hurting. God can and will help you through any struggle you have.

Psalm 118:6 says, "The Lord is for me; I will not fear; What can man do to me?" God will not allow something that a person has said or done to destroy your life. He does not want that to happen. He will help you deal with your pain and move forward. You must be willing to face this pain one more time to give it to God and let Him work in your life.

The healing process also includes learning about the situation in which you were rejected. There are some questions you can ask yourself to begin to get a grasp on the situation:

1. What actually happened that made this person reject me?
2. Is God done with that person in my life, and is it time for me to move on away from them?
3. Is God trying to teach me something by this rejection?
4. Have I forgiven that person? If not, why not?
5. Did I sin against that person, and do I need to go and ask for forgiveness from them?

Depending on how you answered one or more of these questions depends on your next step. If you need to ask for forgiveness, I would suggest you find a way to go and make it right with them. If that person is no longer alive, then you need to find a way to find forgiveness in your heart for the hurt you may have caused that person. It is possible they rejected you because you had hurt them.

If this person rejected you and you cannot find a reason that they did, you should ask God what He wants you to learn from this rejection. It is possible that God wants to move you away from this person and wants to use you in a whole new way. Humans are creatures of habit, and when we get comfortable, we do not move. God wants us to move, and sometimes, the only way He gets us going is to use another to give us a push. This is not always pleasant, but it is effective.

I can think of a couple of times over the years that God moved me away from people who were actually detrimental to me, but I was so used to them I never realized how much they were standing in the way of my service to God. When they rejected me, it hurt deeply, and I can tell you that these times were some of the most painful times I have experienced.

However, looking back, I see it was the only way God could do what He wanted to with me. I would never have left these people on my own. If these people had stayed in my life, I would not be where I am today. I am glad that God moved them even though these were some of the most painful times of my life.

God could also be teaching you forgiveness to those who have rejected you. The focus of our trials is to make us to be like Jesus Christ. As He was rejected and continued to serve God, should we not be able to do the same? The answer is yes, we can. Forgiveness can be difficult for anyone who has been wronged, rejected, or hurt. It is possible to do. One must set their hearts on Jesus and allow Him to help us through our pain.

When reading through the Bible, one can see that Jesus touched hearts everywhere He went. John 16:33 tells us how much Jesus wants us to rest in His arms: "These things I have spoken to you, so that in Me you may have peace. In the world you have tribulation, but take courage; I have overcome the world." I do not know about you, but this Scripture gives me a lot of encouragement!

Finally, sometimes the answer is that there is no answer when we are rejected. We are all sinners, and people can be cold and hurtful. It does not get much simpler than that. There are some people in this world who just hurt other people, and they go through life leaving a lot of damage in their wake. It is nothing else but sin and sin alone, and that is why they rejected you.

We do not always know what the other person is going through when they reject us either. There could be so much turmoil in their lives that they are just lashing out at the people who are closest to them. As we do not always communicate our hurts with others, this is a possibility.

I can prove this statement by asking you a simple question: when you see someone and ask them how they are doing, how do they respond? Without knowing you, or them, I can tell you they probably say they are doing fine. You have probably done the same when someone asks you how you are doing.

We need to be more open and honest in this world today; if you are hurting, it is fine to tell them that you are. This is especially true in marriages and close personal relationships. If people do not know that you are hurting, how can they pray for you and help you? They cannot, and then this pain leads to you not wanting to be around anyone and isolating yourself, and the other person feels rejected. A lot of hurt can be avoided by being honest when someone you are close to asks you how you are doing. If you are hurting, tell them.

A few years ago, I was going through an exceptionally painful time in my life. I had been rejected by a number of people whom I had been serving with for many years. A week after this rejection, someone came up to me in church and asked me how I was doing. I told them I was not doing well, and they offered to pray for me. I accepted.

However, a member of church leadership heard me say that I was not doing well, and they told me that I should not tell anyone about my hurt. He was very animate about me never telling anyone about my pain. I walked away from that conversation devastated. Are we not supposed to carry each other's burdens? Paul believes that we should, and in Galatians 6:2 he tells us so: "Bear one another's burdens, and thereby fulfill the law of Christ." We need to help each other through the pain of rejection.

There can be a fear of sharing rejection with your spouse. You might be thinking that if you share this rejection with your spouse that they will reject you also for the same reason, if you know why you were rejected in the first place. Do not allow the past to creep into your present and affect your future. Give your spouse the chance to share their fears and pain of rejection with you.

This brings me to one of the most important aspects of this dragon. When your spouse shares this rejection, or rejections, with you, they are hurting and are probably a little scared. Please just listen to them, and then show them compassion. Treat your spouse as you would want to be treated when you share a hurt with them. "Treat others the same way you want them to treat you" (Luke 6:31). That says it all.

This goes for everything in life, but it is especially true for the marriage covenant and sharing hurts and pains. Never jump to any conclusions about why your spouse has been rejected. The worse thing you could say is something hurtful similar to this: "I knew there was something wrong with you, and that is why none of your relationships ever lasted." That statement alone is rejection, and you have just destroyed your spouse. It could be that God was preparing them for the marriage they are in and the other person was not able to help your spouse the way you are.

I did not get married until I was forty years old. My wife has never asked me if there was something wrong with me because I was older and not married yet. That would have caused a discussion—a very interesting one too.

Please show your spouse the compassion that they are looking for by sharing this rejection with you. Once you share this rejection with your spouse and have worked through it, this dragon will retreat. He will be defeated and broken as he heads back to his lair, all because you have shown love and compassion to the hurting spouse.

Discussion Questions for the Dragon of Rejection

1. Are you dealing with any past or present rejections?
2. Have you spoken with your spouse about these rejections? If not, why not?
3. Has your spouse ever rejected you? Have you spoken to them about this rejection?

4. Has your spouse shared a rejection with you? How did you deal with this?
5. What scriptures can the two of you use to defeat a Dragon of Rejection?

Notes

CHAPTER 7

The Dragon of Uncertainty

"Look at the birds of the air, that they do not sow, nor reap nor gather into barns, and yet your heavenly Father feeds them. Are you not worth much more than they? And who of you by being worried can add a single hour to his life?" (Matthew 6:26–27)

Do you worry about tomorrow? According to the Scripture above, there is no need to if you have given your life to Jesus Christ.

If there is a Dragon of Uncertainty in your marriage, there is hope. The Dragon of Uncertainty wishes to make sure you question any part of your future and the future of your marriage.

This dragon is particularly good at what he does. He can sneak up on you when you are just sitting quietly talking to your spouse. He will whisper in your ear something that your spouse does that irritates you. Yes, we all have the ability to irritate our spouse, and we probably do in some way! That "ability" to irritate comes from our personalities and history.

The Dragon of Uncertainty attacks in a couple of different ways. The first way is to get you to question your choice of spouse. When your spouse does something that "bothers" you, this dragon jumps into action and tells you that you made the wrong choice and someone else would not bother you like this. Yes, they would! None of us are perfect, and if you think that your spouse is bothering you, what do you think your spouse thinks about you? Yep, the same thing. You bother them too! At least some things that we do are bothersome to our spouses.

The second way that this dragon attacks us is in our lives. Not knowing what may happen tomorrow in any given situation or circumstance can sometimes give us stress.

The biggest problem with this dragon is that it makes you question everything and, if you are not careful, will get you to worry so much that you cannot think properly. Worry and wrong thoughts will overtake you. This dragon may also bring new people into your life, and not for a positive result.

An example might be if your spouse is speaking to a member of the opposite sex. This dragon shows up, reminding you of your past hurt when your heart was broken by an ex, and then you begin to think that your spouse is starting an affair. Surprisingly, at this time when you are questioning the faithfulness of your spouse, that attractive, friendly person at the local store smiles at you, and the rest is history.

This may sound absolutely crazy, but I have seen it more than once in my life. Yes, it can happen quickly too. The absolute worst part of this is that your spouse has done nothing improperly, and by the time the truth comes out, the damage has been done.

This is why this dragon is so dangerous. He thrives off speculation, not truth. He also feeds off from those past hurts that we have experienced. This is why it is so important to deal with those past hurts as quickly as we can.

This dragon will show up quickly if an unforeseen circumstance shows up in your life. Situations like the loss of job, the death of a family member, children going off to college, an illness, or a number of many other reasons. This dragon will usually attack when you are "weakened" by a circumstance with which you have no control over. This dragon loves to feed off your hurts. He is a difficult dragon to defeat, but he can be beaten.

The first thing to do with this dragon is, as with all dragons, recognize his attack. The reason that this is more difficult than the other dragons is that you are usually in some type of emotionally distressed state. As human creations, we have emotions. God is an emotional being, and He has given us emotions. When something happens that triggers one of the many emotions that we have, this dragon moves in. I have already given you a short list of circumstances that can release this dragon, but let's take a look at this list and how these circumstances can relate to marriage.

If one spouse loses their job, there can be many areas of marriage affected. The Dragon of Uncertainty will come rushing in. There is a mortgage to pay, food to buy, car payments to make, and a host of other regular monthly bills. This can be one of the most emotionally frustrating times for a married couple.

It is important, if this happens, not to panic. The first thing that needs to be done is to stay calm and pray! In James 1:2–4, James writes, "Consider it all joy, my brethren, when you encounter various trials, knowing that the testing of your faith produces endurance. And let endurance have its perfect result, so that you may be perfect and complete, lacking in nothing."

Though this promise is true, I need to warn you that one of the worst things you can do in a time of struggle is to start throwing Scripture at someone who is struggling. This is especially true of a spouse. You are dealing with a person who has just suffered a serious blow to their life, and they are dealing with a broken heart. The last thing they need is someone being the Holy Spirit for them. They already understand the promises of God; what they need is someone to understand their heart. God will comfort them as they go through this struggle.

So many times in my life when I have suffered a hurt good people have come to me with very good intentions, giving me every possible Scripture they can think of. I loved them for doing this, but what I really needed was someone to just sit with me.

Job's friends did one thing right. In Job 2:13, Scripture tells us that when they saw Job struggling with all his physical and emotional pain, they sat with him in silence. They sat for seven days and nights with no one speaking a word because they saw Job's pain was so great.

If those friends had started to give Job Scripture at this time, it would have made matters worse. Job knew that God was with him; he just did not understand why these problems came upon him. He was trying to understand.

The same thing happens in our lives. We may not have the same horrific problems that Job went through, but we all have times in our lives when we question God. This is especially true when something dramatic happens in our lives.

Job's friends kept this dragon at a distance by not saying anything. It is only when they started talking that problems start to happen. In short, Job's friends released the dragon. Though Job constantly professed his innocence, his friends were telling him that he had to be guilty of something.

In a marriage, when one spouse loses their job, the worst thing that can be done is for the other spouse to accuse them of doing something to lose their job. Be careful what you say when one spouse loses their job. They are hurting, and even with good intentions, this dragon can be released quickly.

The death of a family member is another situation where this dragon can show up. Dealing with death is probably the most difficult circumstance that one could deal with. It is also something that when experienced reminds us of our own mortality. The uncertainty of tomorrow can be overwhelming if we allow it to be.

It is important for the spouse who is watching their spouse grieve to be especially careful. I have heard one spouse tell another, "I really did not like the person who died, anyway." What a dangerous and heartless statement. I can tell you that I actually saw the dragon escape and run toward the grieving partner. It was devastating.

Fortunately, this couple attacked the dragon quickly. When the emotions of death surface, the grieving person will not be able to think or act as they usually do. This also applies to the one who is watching their spouse grieve. Emotions happen so quickly that sometimes words cannot be caught before being spoken. Again, this may be one of those times when the one spouse needs to sit in silence.

The one other circumstance that I would like to discuss is illness. When a spouse gets sick, there can be the uncertainty of the future. The uncertainty comes from the thoughts that the one who is sick may never recover fully or that the illness could turn out to be fatal. The effects of this type of circumstance can be devastating, depending on the diagnosis.

When a person becomes ill, it is important to feel the emotions that you have at the time. Please do not ever try to repress the emotions that you are feeling. This is a difficult time, and the uncertainty of an illness should not be ignored.

A few years ago, I become ill. The doctors could not figure what was wrong, and it almost killed me twice. I spent many nights in the emergency room and many days in the doctor's office looking for a diagnosis. I can tell you that I was preparing for the worst.

On Thanksgiving Day 2010, I told my wife that we needed to prepare for my death. I had been sick for over a month, it was getting progressively worse on a daily basis, and it was worsening quickly. The doctors were telling me that it was all in my head and that there was nothing wrong with me. One doctor went so far as to say that I had been so sick for so long that at this point I had actually healed but I did not realize it yet. Really, I was better and did not know it?

My wife was a wreck. We were searching for answers, and we were getting nothing, but that it was all in my head. I was unable to eat much, and I lost over forty pounds in about a month and a half. I actually turned gray, and could not get off the couch most days.

They checked everything they could think of, and I finally was given an ultrasound on my abdomen. It was through this ultrasound that they found gallstones. Being that we had nothing else to go by, the surgeon was the next stop. He removed the gallbladder with all the gallstones, and they also discovered that it was seriously inflamed. If they had not gotten it out when they did, someone else would have written this book.

However, that is not the end of the story. I have some lingering effects of this sickness. They may be with me forever, something that will be up to God if He decides to heal me completely or not. I must do my part as far as eating properly and exercising, but my body took a pretty good beating over those few months.

The Dragon of Uncertainty, when it comes to illness, is one of the most difficult dragons to understand. This difficulty in understanding makes it difficult to slay. When dealing with this dragon, it is important to remember that doctors are as fallible as anyone of us is. It is also important to make sure that you ask lots of questions, and if there are tests that you want, you make sure that the doctor gives you that test. It could be a matter of life or death. We must use God-given wisdom when dealing with medical issues. I am not telling you to go out and verbally abuse your doctor until you get what you want. You treat him or her with the respect he or she deserves, but make sure that you are your own patient advocate.

Now for the spouse who is the primary caregiver. They are in emotional turmoil. They are watching the person whom they love struggle with illness. It is incredibly demanding on their emotions to watch this occur. The spouse who is sick is going to be short–tempered, and if the illness goes on for a time, they may actually get to the point where they will take their anger and frustration out on their spouse.

This is a dangerous dragon and does not die easily. The problem with this dragon is that the longer the illness goes on, the bigger and more dangerous it becomes. The best way to slay this dragon is to attack it head-on. This dragon will do what it can to make sure that the anger, fear, and frustration that both spouses are feeling continues on. It is the married couple's responsibility to do everything in their power to stay calm and deal with the illness as best they can.

Again, it is important to not hide your feelings and emotions. I would go so far as to say that you should discuss the illness with each other. This is a major situation that is occurring, and it is a part of your marriage for the time that the illness goes on. If there is anything you get from this chapter, it needs to be this: do not ignore the illness, ever! This is especially true if the illness has the possibility of being fatal.

I am not telling you to give up hope; I am just telling you to use wisdom. I believe that God heals, but I also believe that God does not heal everyone. Many people in the Bible suffered with physical ailments, and not all were healed. Use wisdom, never give up hope, and hold on to God. God cares for you, and He has His hands on you and on your situation.

Discussion Questions for the Dragon of Uncertainty

1. Are you dealing with any type of uncertainty in your life and marriage today?
2. Have you spoken with your spouse about any uncertainty you may be facing?

3.   Are you dealing with any uncertainty with an illness? If so, have you shared your feelings and thoughts with your spouse?

4.   Have there been any emotional events in your life that have left you open for the Dragon of Uncertainty to find a weakness and way into your life and marriage?

5.   What scriptures can the two of you use to defeat a Dragon of Uncertainty?

Notes

CHAPTER 8

The Dragon of Lying

"There are six things which the Lord hates, Yes, seven which are an abomination to Him: Haughty eyes, a lying tongue, and hands that shed innocent blood, a heart that devises wicked plans, Feet that run rapidly to evil, a false witness who utters lies, and one who spreads strife among brothers."
(Proverbs 6:16–19)

In this passage, the things that God hates are mentioned, and lying is so hated by God that He mentions it twice. Why do you think that is?

A marriage has a foundation of love, respect, and honesty from both spouses. There is never a fifty-fifty situation in marriage. It is always 100 percent from each spouse, and nothing less.

In this section, I want to focus on the honesty part of marriage. It's going to be uncomfortable for some of you at first, but give me a chance to get through my thoughts.

Have any of you ever been falsely accused of something in your marriage or in relationships before you were married? Have you ever been lied to in your marriage or relationships? Personally, I believe that there is nothing worse. I have been in a relationship where I was accused of being unfaithful. I was working so much that even if I wanted to be unfaithful I would not have had the time. I explained to this person that I was not in any other relationship but ours. She refused to believe me no matter what I said.

However, what was interesting was that *she* was being unfaithful to *me*. She used to tell me all the time that the person doing the accusing of being unfaithful was the one who was being unfaithful. I guess she was right.

Here is a question: why did she not just tell me that she wanted to leave the relationship? It would have saved so much pain in our lives if she had just been honest. Honesty may hurt at first, but at least when you tell the truth, the person hearing it can work through what they need to work through. Maybe you have experienced something like this also.

This dragon is one that Satan loves to release. In John 8:44, Jesus speaks of Satan and his speech: "You are of your father the devil, and you want to do the desires of your father. He was a murderer from the beginning, and does not stand in the truth because there is no truth in him. Whenever he speaks a lie, he speaks from his own nature, for he is a liar and the father of lies."

Jesus is speaking to the religious leaders of the day, but He specifically mentions Satan and how his speech is filled with lies. Looking at Satan throughout the Bible, we see he has lied from the beginning of time. I call this "Twisted Scripture." Satan will take God's own words, put his spin on them, and possibly deceive us. Deception is still a lie, and according to Jesus, Satan is the father of lies.

Some of you may be thinking that I am calling your spouse the devil because they may have lied to you in the past. Not exactly what I am saying. It is more that if your spouse does lie to you, they are *acting* like the devil. That may sound harsh, but when lies infiltrate a marriage, there is nothing positive that can come from it. Only when the truth is told, forgiveness is asked for, and forgiveness is granted will the marriage have a chance to move forward.

There is one very important component to this issue that needs to be addressed. As with all sin, once forgiveness is asked for and granted, the issues should not be brought up again. At this point, reliving the situation will only hurt, not help. There may be a time when the situation needs to be discussed when you are both ready to talk it over.

Also, there are going to be many emotions that will need to be dealt with by the spouse who has been lied to. This spouse will need time to work through all these emotions. Depending on the lies that were told, it may take a great deal of time to work through the emotions.

Please be patient with your spouse as they do. Remember, you have just admitted to lying to your spouse about something, and they are probably in shock. You also need to know—I do not know how to say this any other way—you have caused this problem as the spouse who has lied, and there will be consequences to this sin. One of those consequences may be that your spouse wants nothing to do with you for a day or two. Show them love, and give them time to process what has just happened.

A lie does not have to, and should not, destroy a marriage. I know marriages that have lived through the lie of adultery and actually became stronger. I am not saying to go out and have an affair to strengthen your marriage—that is just foolishness—but if you have lied to your spouse, know it is not the end. You just have to give yourself time to work through it.

If you are about to lie to your spouse, let me ask you a question: "Why are you going to lie to the one person you can trust more than anyone else on the planet?" If you follow through on this sin, you will have a major hurdle to overcome when the truth finally comes out.

The truth will find a way, and you will have an incredibly difficult situation on your hands.

You should be able to tell your spouse anything. If you have struggles, tell them. It may be difficult and it may shock them, but your spouse needs to know what is going on in your life so that they can come alongside of you and help you. The best accountability partner you have is your spouse.

You may be thinking that your spouse would never be that understanding if you told them the truth about a particular situation. Truth is still the best way to go. Give them the chance to hear what you have to say, and then work through it.

If you are the one who has a spouse coming to you with a struggle and they need to talk to you about it, let me give you some thoughts on this. Please be patient and understanding with them. They are obviously struggling to the point where they are ready to lie to you, and the worse thing you can do is to lose your mind over the conversation.

All of us have struggles and problems we deal with; please do not forget this when your spouse comes to you with their problem. One day, it could be you who may have to go to your spouse, and how would you want them to react to you and your struggles? You would want them to listen and give you their heart. Please give them the same.

Jesus tells us in John 8:32, "And you will know the truth, and the truth will make you free." He is speaking about revelation about Himself, but by application, we can use this Scripture to make sure that our lines of communication stay open and the Dragon of Lying stays in his lair.

Nothing good will come out of lying to your spouse. It will only cause problems, and depending on the intensity of the lie and how long the deceit has gone on for, it could take some time for your marriage to recover. Please just remember the Scripture that I gave you at the beginning of this chapter. God hates a lying tongue, and so should you.

Discussion Questions for the Dragon of Lying

1. Are you considering lying to your spouse about something?
2. Have you already lied to your spouse, and what are you going to do next about correcting it?
3. Has you spouse lied to you and asked for forgiveness? Did you grant forgiveness? Why or why not?
4. What scriptures can the two of you use to defeat a Dragon of Lying?

Notes

CHAPTER 9

The Dragon of Secrets

"For God will bring every act to judgment, every-thing which is hidden, whether it is good or evil."
(Ecclesiastes 12:14)

I have heard it said that not telling someone the whole story is as bad as lying. Some would say that it is a form of lying. Either way, keeping secrets from your spouse can be a dangerous game, and a game that will never be won.

In the last chapter, we discussed the Dragon of Lying and the problem it can cause in marriages. This chapter will look at what happens when you release the Dragon of Secrets in a marriage.

Looking at the Scripture for this chapter, one can see that God knows all that is hidden and will one day bring judgment to every act. The part that should concern us is the word *hidden* and what that represents.

If we apply that word to this chapter, one could see that God will one day judge every deed, whether it is good or evil. If you think you can hide something from God, you are sadly mistaken. If you are hiding something from your spouse, you are headed for disaster.

Misty and I both meet with people privately, and we also meet with couples collectively. The one rule that I put into place is that we will use confidentially when meeting one-on-one with someone who has requested some form of counsel with us. The only thing I ask her when she gets home is if there is anything I need to know to pray about. She either says yes or no. I have the same rule when I meet with someone.

The reason I am telling you this is that I want you to understand that there is a difference between keeping confidentiality and keeping a secret. There is a huge difference in these two definitions. When someone meets with us, they can assume confidentiality, unless they tell us that a law has been broken or is about to be broken. I never want a person to be uncomfortable thinking that we are talking about them with each other.

We have both asked the person we are meeting with if we can share something we have heard if we need a male or female perspective. Depending on their answer depends on whether or not we discuss the situation with each other. There is nothing wrong with this. Proverbs 11:13 says, "He who goes about as a talebearer reveals secrets, but he who is trustworthy conceals a matter." I want people to know they are safe with either Misty or myself. We can only help if they communicate with us, and if they do not trust us, they will not open up to us.

I have seen secrets come very close to destroying a marriage. I am not talking about hiding an adulterous affair, though that can be a huge problem; I am talking about other situations. Situations like finances can be an issue. If you are spending money and not telling your spouse, it will come out eventually. According to the Bible, we are one flesh (Mark 10:8): whatever one owns, the other owns.

Husband and wife are considered one flesh in God's eyes. So it is important to make sure that we act as one. We should always respect our spouse and talk to them about whatever is happening n our lives. The second we stop talking and stop sharing the events in our lives, we start to call out a Dragon of Communication. Remember, communication can be silence.

Secrets have no place in a marriage. Period. If there is something that you are not telling your spouse, you may want to stop and ask yourself why. Are you trying to protect them by not telling them something? Are you afraid to tell your spouse something? If so, you are now asking for a Dragon of Secrets to appear. There should be nothing that you would not share with your spouse. If I am purposely hiding something from Misty, then we have a problem. There should be nothing that I cannot share with her in our marriage.

Look at it this way: how would you feel if it was your spouse not telling you something? Would you be concerned that there is something more to what they are not telling you? As soon as one Dragon of Secrets appears, there is a very good chance that he will bring along a few of his friends. Now you have a horde of this type of dragon, and it can quickly get out of hand. When there is one secret, just as if there were one lie, there needs to be others to cover up the first one. It makes more sense that no secret is kept to begin with.

There are other situations that may release this dragon. If one of you has a past that you have struggles with because of sins or choices, please tell your spouse. If this secret is kept, then the Dragon of Past Hurts may appear along with the Dragon of Secrets. Please share whatever you need to with your spouse so you can move forward in your marriage. This could include sexual abuse or some form of addiction.

Another secret that some have tried to keep is the loss of a job. I have no idea how someone would have been able to keep this one a secret, but it has been attempted before. I have been fired from only one job in my life, and as soon as it occurred, I told my wife. I knew that we needed to take some action and put a budget plan into action, and we had to do it quickly. We were not in panic mode, but we had to use wisdom so that we could pay our bills. If I did not tell her when it happened, it would have been disastrous for us.

You may think that is hype, but let me tell you why it was important for me to tell her. At the time I called to tell her I had been terminated, she was on the phone with a loan officer, and we were in talks to get money to put an addition on our home. She had to put me on hold and tell the loan officer that we had just had an unexpected loss of job and we would have to wait.

If I had waited to tell her, or not told her at all, she would have gone through with the loan. There would have been no way to pay back that money without my job, and we would have probably lost our home. Secrets destroy, and had I kept this from her, it would have destroyed much.

The secret of financial issues can be one that is devastating to the marriage. This could be some debt that has been incurred before marriage and one spouse does not tell the other that there is this huge debt that they have. It comes out one day, and then there has to be a debt payoff plan that needs to be put in place. If the debt is high enough, it could now affect the couple's credit ratings for their future together. This would not necessarily mean that their credit ratings would be in trouble forever, but it may make it difficult to purchase a home or car in the immediate future.

Another financial secret could be if the husband or wife was spending foolishly without the knowledge of the other. This has happened to more than one couple I know. It is extremely hurtful to their spouse, and in at least one instance I know, the couple has not recovered from it financially. The uncovering of one of these secrets was over five years ago and destroyed their retirement account. The husband had been saving his whole life, and their savings account was wiped out.

Couples should be planning for their financial future, not destroying it. If couples would share the financial responsibility, or at least know what their financial situation is, there should not be a financial problem.

In our marriage, Misty handles the finances, but I know how much money we have and how much goes out. She is phenomenal at numbers, and she uses this gift handling our money.

Another secret that can be damaging to the marriage is the secret of health. If you are hiding a health issue from your spouse, you are being cruel. I understand that the Dragon of Uncertainty can be released with a health issue, but if you hide this from your spouse, you now have the Dragon of Secrets coming alongside of the Dragon of Uncertainty. If you are not speaking to your spouse about this, the Dragon of Communication has now entered the mix, and you have a serious battle that will need to take place to slay this group of dragons. Again, it is easier to be honest and open with your spouse, or fiancé, so that these dragons do not show up.

Health issues can be difficult to discuss, especially if it is something as sensitive as infertility or a health issue that has been going on for some time. It can be difficult to talk about health issues, but would it not be better to tell your spouse so you can deal with it together? The answer is yes.

One other secret that I would like to address would be if there is a problem or concern in the marriage covenant and you have not shared your heart with your spouse. If you are holding anything back from your spouse, now is the time to share that concern. Secrets do not have to be something you have recently been involved in. Some people take years to divulge something that is bothering them in the marriage. This will slow the growth of the marriage, as there will always be this "thing" that is hanging over the couple.

As I have already discussed the importance of communication, it should seem that sharing is a great idea within the marriage covenant. It may be that you are concerned that if you share this particular thing that your spouse will become angry about the problem that you are having. It could be that you grew up in a house where no one shared problems within the marriage and just ignored some of those problems and hoped they would just go away.

I can tell you that unless a dragon is faced head-on, it will not go away without leaving some damage. If the dragon is completely ignored, it may never go away completely. It will just sit and wait until it has the opportunity to attack again.

Secrets in marriage are never a great idea. Husband and wife should be open and honest with each other, starting with the dating period. The Dragon of Secrets is one who works in the shadows and will divide the husband and wife by telling one of them that keeping a secret from their spouse is something that they should be doing. Do not believe this lie. Share your struggles, problems, and concerns with your spouse.

Discussion Questions for the Dragon of Secrets

1. Are you keeping any secrets that you have in your marriage right now?
2. Is there something in your past that is painful that you have not shared with your spouse yet?
3. Are you concerned how your spouse will respond if you share that secret with them?
4. Have you thought about the repercussions that keeping a secret might have in your marriage?
5. Has your spouse recently shared a secret that they have been keeping? How did you react?
6. If God was to reveal what you have kept "hidden," what would be the result?

7. What scriptures can the two of you use to defeat a Dragon of Secrets?

Notes

CHAPTER 10

The Dragon of Unforgiveness

"Then Peter came and said to Him, 'Lord, how often shall my brother sin against me and I forgive him? Up to seven times?' Jesus said to him, 'I do not say to you, up to seven times, but up to seventy times seven.'" (Matthew 18:21–22)

One of the hardest things we are asked to do is to forgive another when they hurt us. Not only does Jesus command us to forgive, but also He tells us to forgive over and over again. There is never a time when we should not forgive another. This is especially true when our spouse hurts us.

When our spouse says or does something that hurts us deeply, we must find a way to forgive them. I will repeat the statement that none of us are perfect, but we are perfect sinners. All of us will say or do something at some time in our lives that will hurt our spouse. As we are all imperfect creatures, we will stumble and say foolish things. It is a given. However, it is up to us to be willing to forgive at any given second.

Each of us reacts differently to a hurt. Some of those reactions that may overtake us would be getting angry, feeling frustrated, retreating in silence, crying, screaming, and doing a host of other reactions. Please notice that one of the first reactions that we may have does not include forgiveness. Yet this is what Jesus says we should be ready to do seven times seventy times.

Some of you may be counting until your spouse hits that 490 mark, but that is not what Jesus is saying. He is simply stating that no matter how many times someone sins against you, forgiveness must always be granted. Even if the person who has done the offending has not asked for forgiveness, your heart must always be ready to forgive.

I would like you to know that I am not condoning abusive behavior here. If you are in an abusive relationship, please seek professional help now! Do not stay in a marriage that has turned abusive. There is never a reason to raise a hand in anger toward another human being, ever! By seeking professional help, you will be able to figure out the root issues and then make a decision, along with the help of a professional counselor, on your next steps.

What I am saying is that we need to have understanding with our spouses. If something is said or done that offends us, we should communicate that with our spouse. Sometimes we say or do things without even knowing we are offending our spouse. We just did not understand that we have hurt them.

I can tell you that you will find out very quickly if you have said something that has brought them pain. Everyone has a way to display hurt, and most of us are quite willing to display that hurt. This is especially true if you want to immediately get revenge for the pain.

When communicating a specific hurt with the spouse who has done the offense, we should always approach them with love and gentleness. Coming at your spouse in a rage will do nothing to help the situation. It will certainly help escalate it, though! Remember how you would want to be treated in this situation. If you have offended your spouse, you should always be ready to ask them for forgiveness the second you have recognized the hurt. By asking for forgiveness and being granted forgiveness, your marriage will become stronger.

When this dragon appears, the quickest way to defeat him would be to forgive the offending spouse. As soon as forgiveness is granted, this dragon will crawl back to its lair. It is when forgiveness is not asked for, or is not granted, that this dragon will grow stronger and get angrier.

This is one dragon that does not leave too quickly once it is released. As unforgiveness can sink deep into one's heart, the chances of this dragon continuing its rampage once it is released are high. This dragon will eat a person who fails to, or refuses, to forgive. Each day that goes by without forgiveness will cause the person who has refused to grant forgiveness to continue to hurt.

Jesus gives us a warning in Matthew 6:14–15 about forgiving another: "For if you forgive others for their transgressions, your heavenly Father will also forgive you. But if you do not forgive others, then your Father will not forgive your transgressions." Not only does Jesus tell us to forgive, but also He tells us to forgive others each time someone sins against us. How powerful!

The entire Bible has a foundation of forgiveness throughout it. As Jesus hangs on the cross, the first thing He says is, "Father, forgive them, they know not what they do." Here is the most innocent of all dying for all of us. He has been falsely accused. He has been beaten. He has been nailed to a cross.

Through the accusations, the beatings, and being nailed to a cross, the first thing Jesus does is forgive those who are killing Him. After thinking about this, how important do you think forgiveness is to God? Without forgiveness, none of us would experience salvation. Without forgiveness, you will experience struggles in your life. Without forgiveness, you will experience struggles in your marriage. Forgiveness is key to a strong marriage and Christian life.

Some of you may have been hurt deeply by your spouse, very deeply, and you are wondering how you can ever forgive them. You need to say it first, then you need to get the emotions you are experiencing under control. It takes time for this to happen. As I have said in previous chapters, we must be patient with our spouses, and this is especially true when they sin against us. This dragon wants you to hold on to anger, bitterness, and unforgiveness. Please do not feed this dragon by doing so.

Some of you may be struggling with this now as your spouse has committed some sin that you feel should never be forgiven. First, look back at the scriptures that I have already shared. Second, what if it was you who needed forgiveness? Would you want your spouse to forgive you? I am sure the answer is yes.

Please do not let the bitterness of unforgiveness get a hold of you and keep you enslaved to it. Forgive the one who has offended you, ask God to help you deal with the emotions of the hurt, and then move forward to a stronger marriage.

The Dragon of Unforgiveness can also be released in a marriage by a situation that may have happened outside of the marriage. Somewhere in your life, someone may have hurt you, and you bring that hurt into your marriage. This type of dragon can be a bit more difficult to defeat, as it may have been an incident that happened so many years ago. If this incident were severe, you may have trouble forgiving the person, or persons, who have hurt you.

As this dragon has been free for so long, you will have a difficult time slaying this dragon. It may actually be part of your life, and as you are comfortable with it, you may not want to rid yourself of it. I would suggest that you do. The forgiveness must come from you and toward the person who has hurt you. If this person is no longer alive or you know you will never hear from this person, you can set your heart on forgiving them right where you are. It can be difficult but not impossible. Once you free yourself from this, you can move forward in your marriage and your life, as you have freed yourself from this hurt.

One thing that is important to remember about forgiveness is that it is not a sign of weakness. It is actually the opposite. Those who forgive show a strength that does not come naturally as the world tells us that we should hold grudges and get even. Jesus never told us to forgive once; He told us to forgive over and over again. It would benefit us greatly to take heed in what He said and forgive those who have hurt us, even if they have hurt us repeatedly.

Discussion Questions for the Dragon of Unforgiveness

1. Have you sinned against your spouse and not asked for forgiveness?
2. Have you been asked to forgive and not granted it because you feel that the sin was too great?
3. Are you holding anything against your spouse even though you have forgiven them?
4. What are some of the ways you can deal biblically with your emotions after you have been sinned against and all has been forgiven?
5. What scriptures can the two of you use to defeat a Dragon of Unforgiveness?

Notes

CHAPTER 11

The Dragon of Children

"Behold, children are a gift of the Lord, the fruit of the womb is a reward." (Psalm 127:3)

It might seem strange that I would say that there is a dragon that has to deal with children, but please let me explain.

First, I want to say that my heart goes out to those of you who have not been able to conceive a child. Your pain must be excruciating. My wife and I are physically unable to have children, so we have an idea of what it must be like for those of you who share this struggle with us. Please understand that just because you have not been able to have a child does not mean that God does not love you any less. Sin has taken over the world, and not being able to conceive is just one of the sin curses that we carry. I know that is probably little comfort for you, but there is nothing I can say that will lessen this particular pain. I wish there were words that would.

Second, some of you may have lost children through miscarriage, abortion, or some other situation. Please know that my heart goes out to you also. I personally was involved in an abortion before I began my relationship with Jesus Christ. I understand some of the pain that an abortion brings. Only through God's grace and plan of salvation did I get through that time. We have felt the pain of a miscarriage as my wife and I experienced that years ago. I cannot think of anything more painful than the loss of a child. I grieve with you.

I would also like to say that this chapter will discuss many of the conversations I have had with parents. Though these words may seem like the parent is having, or has had, second thoughts about having children, this is far from the truth. Every single parent whom I have spoken with would have more children. Some did! Looking back at the Scripture above, one can see that God sees children as a blessing. These parents all did too.

Finally, it must seem quite odd that throughout the Bible, God says and shows that children are a blessing and a gift. As this is truth, how can there be a Dragon of Children?

When a child is born, the parents of this child are excited about being parents, especially for the first time. However, there needs to be some serious schedule changes to the new parents' life, so they make sure they get some sleep, eat, exercise, and spend time with each other. Sounds simple, right? Not even close! Every time I have asked a group of married people what the biggest change in their lives have been, the topic of children is mentioned. Every. Single. Time.

Here is where the Dragon of Children shows up. When a parent holds their child for the first time, all kinds of emotions rush in. Most of these emotions are positive as the excitement of bringing this new life into the world sets in. Soon, reality shows up, and the usual schedule of their lives is turned upside down. Sleep becomes something that the parents long for. Being able to go out for dinner becomes a chore, or an impossibility, as the babysitter may not be available at the last minute. The idea of a vacation now becomes an adventure of seeing how much "baby stuff" one can fit into a car.

One couple I knew said they refused to give up their dinner date that they had on a weekly basis after they had children. They continued their weekly dinner date, and though they did, some things still changed. They had to make sure that they had packed all the items needed for their new baby with them. What was once a simple dinner for two had now become a not-so-simple dinner for three.

The best way to explain this dragon would be that this dragon is one of change. Quick change. Though a child is carried for about nine months, the change of birth can come quickly. One day, there is no baby; the next day, there is another little person in your home needing your attention.

Most people do not like change. In fact, most people dislike it greatly. However, the Dragon of Children will be one of change for many years to come. This is where people can get a bit nervous and allow the Dragon of Children to cause issues in their marriage.

Once a couple brings a new life into this world, there are many facets of their lives that will be affected. Finances, time, work, sleep, exercise, hobbies, and families are just some of the parts of their lives that will be touched. None of these by themselves may be a problem, but when you touch on every single part of your life that needs some form of change, it can be confusing, tiring, and frustrating.

Once a baby comes into your home, there will also be an unending parade of good-hearted people coming to your home to help you. Each of them will be more than willing to offer advice on how to raise your children, and some of them will probably tell you that you are not parenting them correctly. With this being said, let's look at some of the changes that will come into your life after you bring your baby home.

Change 1: lots of people will be visiting. Remember all those people at your wedding asking when you are going to start having babies? Well, they will now be at your house telling you how to raise your new child. You are probably going to be exhausted when you bring the new baby home, and it will be necessary that you stay calm and connected with your spouse.

If you and your spouse are private people, the constant flow of traffic into your home may be disorienting. It may actually be something that may anger you. Please remember that they are only trying to share your enthusiasm with the new member of your family. They will also leave you and your spouse with a very tired baby when they leave and return to their homes.

Change 2: those spontaneous dates that you enjoyed so much may not happen. When there were just the two of you and all you needed to do was figure out where you wanted to go and eat, this will now require either a babysitter or a whole bunch of "baby accessories" to go along with you. It may take so much work that after a day of working and taking care of the baby, you just may want to stay home.

Please remember that your marriage is still important. Do not forget to keep the marriage in focus, and your spouse will still need to be loved through all this change. It will be difficult, but it will not be impossible.

Change 3: those yearly vacations will now be a whole new adventure. Many people I know sold their cars to buy one of these "cool minivans" to hold all new things for the new member of the family. As a side note, let me tell you the minivan was designed by a genius. Two huge doors on either side—awesome!

Anyway, buying one of these vehicles can be such a change for people that they struggle to drive one. Please do not be offended, but if you are struggling driving one of these, note it is a pride issue. However, once you get the vacation thing down with your new child, it can be amazing. There are so many family places to go these days, and many are within driving distance of many major cities.

Do not give up your vacation; just be adaptable to new and exciting things for your family to do and experience. I cannot tell you how many times I have talked to children at the places my wife and I have traveled to. They are a blessing to be around.

Change 4: finances. It may seem that every penny you spend will be spent on your child. Might be some truth in that. There will be clothes (that the child will probably quickly outgrow), medicine, doctor's visits, and hospital costs for delivering the child, maybe the cost of a new minivan, cost for baby furniture, babysitters, baby food, diapers, and a host of other items.

It will be imperative to make sure that you have adjusted your budget the best that you can to prepare for the baby before it is born. If you wait too long, the Dragon of Money shows up (we will address him later in the book) and, along with the Dragon of Children, will wreak havoc in your home.

Change 5: shock and fear. We're pregnant! How do you feel when you hear that from your own mouth? It is a life-changing statement. I once worked at a hospital, and a family came in. The mother seemed very excited, as did her children. I noticed the father was not looking so well, and I thought it was going to be him who was coming in for the testing.

When I went to see who my next patient was, it turned out to be her, the mother. I was somewhat confused, as the father was looking worse by the minute. When I looked at the tests her doctor was requesting, I noticed the tests were prenatal work. She was pregnant and very excited. Her husband was not as excited, and it showed.

When the family came into the room, the mother could not contain her excitement and was just talking very quickly, and finally, she blurted this out, "I just found out I'm pregnant, and it's twins!"

There are a couple of other factors you should know about here. First, they already had three children with them. Second, she was forty-three years old. Fortunately, she was healthy, and there were no concerns at the time of this testing.

I felt I needed to talk to the husband, as he really did not look well. All I could get out of him was, "We are having two of them. I'm too old to have twins." There was zero excitement from him. He was in shock, and did not know what to do. She was completely lost in her excitement and was not afraid to show it to anyone. He was probably preparing for the next part of their lives together and all of a sudden he is hit with a pregnancy that is resulting in twins.

I am sure a Dragon of Children showed up on this family's life along the way. I never saw this couple again, but I do hope that it all worked out for them. I am pretty confident that this man eventually overcame the shock of this pregnancy. He showed love to his children even though he was in shock, and I am sure that once he got over that initial shock he finally shared the joy of the twins.

Fear is another emotion that this dragon can cause and use. This is especially true for the first child, or if there may be some questions on the health of the baby. If you are about to become parents for the first time, know this can be somewhat of a fearful time.

The Bible tells us to not be afraid in Isaiah 41:10: "Do not fear, for I am with you; Do not anxiously look about you, for I am your God. I will strengthen you, surely I will help you, surely I will uphold you with My righteous right hand." How many parents have prayed this Scripture back to God at 3:00 a.m., wanting their child to go back to sleep? How many parents have prayed this Scripture back to God when the medical reports of their child came back with some concerns?

Fear can be all consuming, and in situations with a medical concern, this fear can be overpowering. God wants us to trust Him, and though sin is what has caused us problems like sickness, He still wants us to hold on to Him through the trial.

Change 6: exhaustion. I have heard parent after parent tell me how tired they are and the "tired" that they are experiencing is like nothing that they have ever experienced before. Lack of sleep can lead to many different issues: memory struggles, illness, being short-tempered, and a host of other problems. It is so imperative that you and your spouse work together to make sure that your schedule works for both of you and the child. If you have more than one child, you now need to make a schedule with the new baby, a schedule that does not take so much time from both of that you are ignoring the other child or children in the home.

Change 7: favoritism. This particular attack from the Dragon of Children will arise if you show favoritism toward one child. As for the other changes, eventually you will get on a schedule that will work for all of you. When parents show favoritism toward one child, it can lead to a disaster.

God warns us about favoritism in the book of James and in family history in Genesis. James 2:1 says, "My brethren, do not hold your faith in our glorious Lord Jesus Christ with an attitude of personal favoritism." James continues in chapter 2, verse 9, "But if you show partiality, you are committing sin and are convicted by the law as transgressors."

If you favor one child over another, you are in sin, and nothing good will come from it. If you show favoritism, the Dragon of Children may stay with your family for years.

In the story of Abraham, Abraham favors one son over the other. Abraham chose Isaac over Ishmael. Isaac then chooses Esau, and Jacob suffers the favoritism of his brother over him. This favoritism continues in the story of Jacob. As Jacob saw favoritism from the time he was a boy from his father Isaac, Jacob continues this horrific trait and favors Joseph. This favoritism causes Joseph a trip to an empty well and then into slavery in Egypt courtesy of his brothers, who have watched the favoritism Joseph received from his father. God eventually repaired this fractured relationship between Joseph and his family, but it was years of waiting and suffering before the reconciliation occurred.

Looking at this biblical story, one can see how much damage favoritism toward one child can do. The devastation to a child who is watching their brother or sister be favored can be far-reaching and long-lasting. I would beg you to stop favoring one child over another if you are. Allow your children to use the gifts God has given them, and feed those gifts and talents.

It would do all parents well to follow Proverbs 22:6: "Train up a child in the way he should go, even when he is old he will not depart from it." That is for all children, not the one(s) a parent thinks has better gifts. Never, ever favor a child over another.

There is one another attack that this dragon will use. This attack is where one spouse wants children and the other does not. This type of discussion should take place during the dating relationship, when it looks as though there is a future for the couple. However, sometimes ideas change after marriage. Premarital counseling should always be required, as topics like this will be addressed.

If there is a difference of opinion on whether or not the husband or wife wants children, it should be addressed immediately. This may require a third-party counselor to work through the issues. This is a very difficult attack from this dragon to deal with in this type of book, but praying together about this would be the first step I would suggest. Then you may need to go seek counseling from someone where you live so you can talk it through with a mediator.

Finally, there is an attack from this dragon that is not often spoken about: this would be a pregnancy that occurs before marriage. Yes, Christians can find themselves in this situation as easily as anyone else. Sexual temptation is out there, and if it gets a hold of someone and temptation leads to sin, pregnancy can occur.

If this is to happen, there will be many emotions that will have to be dealt with quickly. The one thing that is not an option in this type of situation is an abortion. Taking the life of an unborn child is never an option. Most of us are familiar with the Ten Commandments in the Book of Exodus. Exodus 20:13 says, "You shall not murder." As lovingly as I can say this, abortion *is* murder. You are having a baby killed in the womb. I know that may not be a popular comment in today's society, but it is not society that makes the rules—God does.

If you have found yourself in a situation where there is a child conceived from a premarital sexual encounter, it is important to think about your health and the health of the child. Get to a doctor. You may be embarrassed or feel ashamed, but you need to get to a doctor to make sure everything is fine. If you need someone to talk to get to your local church, make an appointment to talk with your pastor, and ask for help.

Depending on your situation, and you do not want to keep the child, adoption is the best option. There are plenty of people who are desperate to have a child and cannot. They would love to give your child a good home. Please understand that giving your child to a loving home does not mean that you are a terrible person and that you do not love your child. It means that because of certain circumstances, you may not be in a position to raise the child.

You may be thinking that you do not want to go through the nine months of carrying the child, but this is part of the consequence of your sin. I cannot say that any other way. Please accept it in the loving way it was meant. You are responsible to take care of that child, and you need to do so. There are a number of organizations that your church can put you in contact with to help you and give you direction for the adoption process.

There will be emotions that you need to deal with in a premarital pregnancy, and it will be a difficult and confusing time. My suggestion to you is to make it right with God first. He knows you are hurting, and He has promised to forgive you of all sins. The verse in 1 John 1:9 tells us, "If we confess our sins, He is faithful and righteous to forgive us our sins and to cleanse us from all unrighteousness." Your sin is not too big for God to forgive; just ask Him. Accept this forgiveness and move forward. It will be a difficult time, but with God and support from others, you will get through this time.

The Dragon of Children can be one of fear, confusion, challenges, and change. For those of you who have children, raise them up in the ways of the Lord. For those of you who are planning on having them, make sure you have discussed the Dragon of Children and the changes that this dragon brings. By careful planning, you can keep this dragon at a distance.

Discussion Questions for the Dragon of Children

1. If you are planning on having children, have you discussed the changes that the Dragon of Children can bring?
2. If you have a child, or children, have you allowed this dragon to creep in?
3. Do you see children as a blessing from God?
4. Have you ever shown one child favoritism over another? What are you doing to correct this?
5. Are you and your spouse in agreement with whether or not you are going to have children? If not, what steps are you taking to work through this?
6. What scriptures can the two of you use to defeat a Dragon of Children?

Notes

CHAPTER 12

The Dragon of the Umbilical Cord

"For this reason a man shall leave his father and his mother, and be joined to his wife; and they shall become one flesh." (Genesis 2:24)

One cannot have children without an umbilical cord. It provides all the nourishment and oxygen that the growing baby needs in the womb. One of the first things that the doctor—or father, in some cases—does is to cut the umbilical cord to release the baby from the mother. Once this cord is cut, the child is now free and begins their growth process outside of the womb.

Can you imagine what would happen if this cord was not cut? The child would grow to be an incredible burden to the parents, especially the mother, and the parents would be an incredible hindrance to the child's growth. Can you see where I may be going here?

After children, the one complaint I have heard is that the parents or the in-laws are interfering with the marriage. This can be due to one of the parents not letting go of the child or one of the children not letting go of their parents. It could also be that the parents or in-laws are just controlling and there would need to be a conversation about boundaries. This is where the Dragon of the Umbilical Cord comes in to do its damage.

Looking at what Moses wrote in Genesis 2:24, one can see how God designed marriage. God wants the married couple to let go of the parents and cleave to each other. This does not mean you are to ignore them completely. As Moses tells us in Exodus 20:12, "Honor you father and your mother, that your days may be prolonged in the land in which the Lord your God gives to you."

We are to enjoy the family unit, but not to the point where it becomes intrusive to the marriage covenant. God feels so strongly about this He makes sure that Jesus and Paul mention it in the New Testament. Jesus speaks it in Matthew 19:5, and Paul repeats it in Ephesians 5:31.

There may be a number of ways that you will define the word *intrusive*. It could be that one set of parents is constantly showing up unexpectedly at your home. You might have parents who are trying to point out how much differently you could be parenting. There is the judgmental parent who may tell you that you are not good enough for their son or daughter. The intrusive parent may also criticize the way you clean your home or your cooking skills.

There are other ways that you may be experiencing this, but the results are all the same. This interference will lead to marriage problems. It does not matter how much love and closeness is in the family; there will be a problem somewhere down the road, especially if it has been going on for a long time and this dragon is not dealt with.

If there is an intrusive parent, it is time for a serious discussion with them. One of the ways to do this would be for the spouse whose parent is unable to cut the umbilical cord to talk to their parents and let them know that they are loved but that the constant presence is not working and the interference is troubling both of you.

This can, and should be, handled in a loving way and not in a way that will hurt or condemn. Just remember to stay calm as you speak with the parent who is the one who is causing the issues. This situation may have been going on for quite some time, and if it took you a few years to get to this point of talking to them, they may be very confused as to why all of a sudden there is a problem. It may be better to have a one-on-one with the parent. If necessary, you can then bring in your spouse for support.

If you are dealing with a "manipulative parent" or a "controlling parent," this advice will be easier said than done. If they try to manipulate or control you, it is best to have your spouse with you at this point. When you sit down as a couple to speak with the parent, or parents, who are causing you an issue, you are showing them that there is a unity within your marriage. This can be a powerful tool, as the parent will see how important this is to both of you.

The action of having both you and your spouse there can speak volumes. It can also make the parent feel as though the two of you are ganging up on them. As you know your parents best, it is something that you will have to decide on how you are going to discuss this concern with them. It is not easy, but it can be done.

I must also address this concern from the child's perspective. As a boy grows up, his father is probably the one whom he will go to in times of need. There are also the boys who will go to their mothers. A lot depends on who may be home at the time.

When I was growing up, the father went off to work and the mother stayed home. Times have changed, and that is not necessarily the case today. When discussing who a girl would go to, one usually believes that they would probably go to their mothers first. However, this is not always the situation.

Arising from which parent the child will go to talk to comes a couple of terms that I have heard, though I do not actually approve of. Mommy's boy and Daddy's girl are terms that are used: the former is for when the male child goes to his mother often, and the latter is used for the females when they constantly go to their father.

I am not attempting to mock these people, I am just using terminology that most people may have heard of and will understand. These types of men and women can be absolutely destructive to a marriage and to their spouse. When a husband or a wife chooses one of their parents over their spouse, big problems can arise.

One of the problems with these two types of people is that these "conditions" may have showed up in the dating relationship and one person thought that after they were married this would change. Worse yet, it could be that one person thought they could change their spouse once they were married. I have seen and heard this more than I care to.

If you are with one of these two types of people, know they will only change if the desire to change is within them. Nothing you can say or do will make them change. This begs the question, "If I cannot change them and they can only change if they want to, what do I do?" You need to help them find the *desire* to change.

Again, this is easier said than done. You will need to talk to your spouse, and this is going to take some time. It may be that no one has ever discussed this with your spouse before. If this is true, then it may be so normal to them that they never knew there was an issue. If this is the only type of relationship they have known with their parents, it will be very uncomfortable for all parties when this discussion takes place. It is all about timing and showing love.

Let's begin with the "Mommy's boy" syndrome. This is the man who cannot let go of his mother and runs to her with every problem he comes up against. He will also run to his mother for advice or share the exciting events in his life with her before going to his wife. The mother also feeds into this situation by making sure she is available often. This type of relationship leaves the man's wife sitting and wondering what she needs to do to get her husband away from his mother and move toward her. This can be frustrating and confusing for her and, if this dragon is not slain quickly, can lead to serious marital problems. The husband escalates these problems as he is the spiritual leader of the home. If this spiritual leader is in the company of his mother more than his wife, this leadership can be nonexistent.

Are there times when a man needs his mother? Of course there are times when he may need a woman's opinion. There is a bond between a mother and any of her children. On the day of my wedding, I was dancing with my mother when she started to cry. She told me that this was harder than the weddings she had attended for either of my sisters. This does not mean that she loves me more than my sisters. I am an only son, and this may have had a deeper effect on her, but it was sweet to hear her say that. She knew that our relationship was going to change, and it did.

I still love my mother deeply, but I married Misty, and she is the woman who is number one in my life now. My mother and I still talk, but not like we used to and not anywhere near what my wife and I do. My mother also understands I am married and Misty comes first.

Something else that helped with this transition was that I had moved out of the house years before I married and I was already independent. I was also raised that if a situation or circumstance came up, I was to handle it on my own. There was no running home for help. To become independent, one must learn to be independent. That may mean tough love is needed. My parents had no problem making sure that I understood it was time to leave the nest. They would look for apartments for me to rent every week, and they made sure that I saw those ads! Believe me when I tell you I received that message loud and clear.

There are also the Daddy's girls who run to Dad for everything. Again, there is a special bond between a father and his daughter, but the women who are constantly running back to Dad may soon find her husband running out of the house.

Misty's dad is very protective of his daughter. I have no problem with this because he still respects that I am her husband and I am the man whom she will come to first. I would have a problem if she were constantly running to him with problems, concerns, or news of the day that she should be sharing with me. I would never stop her from sharing news or asking questions, but there has to be some boundary to what she would talk to her dad about before discussing it with me. She expects the same from me.

If you are in a marriage where your husband or wife is constantly running back to their parents, you are going to need to have a discussion with them about the marriage covenant and how God wants you to live in a marriage. If there is a Dragon of Communication in your marriage, you may have to slay that dragon first before moving forward into this discussion. This can be a very delicate topic, but it still needs to be addressed.

The Dragon of the Umbilical Cord is a dragon that some may fear to go into battle with. As some may not have known any other way of life than to share every life event with their parents, they need to know there needs to be an understanding that this dragon has begun an attack. If the spouse who needs to discuss this situation with their parents has never had to confront them, this is going to be very difficult. This behavior has been normal for them, and they will not be comfortable talking with them about this.

However, it is critical that this dragon is dealt with as soon as it rears its ugly head. This dragon usually attacks at the start of a new marriage. This is when the marriage is at its most vulnerable as the new couple is learning so much about each other and the parents may want to "help" the newlyweds.

If you are a parent reading this book, please allow your married children the space they need to grow together. Love them, make sure they know you are praying for them, but allow them the room to start their marriage. Please cut the umbilical cord so they can grow.

If you are one who runs to one of your parents for everything, please cut the umbilical cord so your marriage can grow. If the umbilical cord is not cut, this dragon will make life very difficult, as you will be dealing with more people than you need to in the marriage.

A marriage is a man and a woman, not a man, woman, and a parent or two.

Discussion Questions for the Dragon of the Umbilical Cord

1. Do either of you have an interfering/manipulating parent?
2. Do either of you need to discuss with your spouse about their relationship with their parent(s)?
3. How difficult will it be for you to have this discussion? Why?
4. Do you put your parents before your spouse?
5. How can you discuss this situation with your parents and still honor them?
6. What scriptures can the two of you use to defeat a Dragon of the Umbilical Cord?

Notes

CHAPTER 13

The Dragon of Money

"For the love of money is a root of all sorts of evil, and some by longing for it have wandered away from the faith and pierced themselves with many griefs." (1 Timothy 6:10)

The Scripture above is so often misquoted and used incorrectly. Money by itself is not evil; it is the *love* of money that is evil. Money is a tool that we use on a daily basis. It is when we abuse this tool that the Dragon of Money will show up and cause damage.

Let me begin by saying I am not against you spending money on recreation, vacations, and other enjoyable things in life. I am saying that if you are working hard to pay your bills and you are in a time where you may be struggling financially, put off some of the wants and focus on the needs you and your family have. Many marriages find themselves in financial distress when they put their wants over their needs.

Creating a simple budget for the home can help slay the Dragon of Money. Most of the computer financial software available today has a budget section in them where you just input the amounts and it will guide you through the budget-making process. These types of programs are great places to start, but one must follow the computer program to have some success.

There are two problems that can occur with money. The first is too little. The second is too much. The latter can be more of a problem if there is a great deal of money that some acquires quickly and that person, or persons, receiving it have no idea how to handle a large sum of money all at once. There is a reason why many people who play the lottery and win large sums of money eventually end up in financial ruins. Too much money gained too quickly is as bad as too much money lost too quickly. Both have results that are horrendous. The Dragon of Money can be either a fast-moving dragon or a slow-moving one. What this means is that money can come very quickly or slowly over a given period of time. It can also be lost in the same manner.

It is important for the husband and wife to discuss their financial situation. It does not matter how much you have, how much debt is involved, or what you want to purchase. Money must be discussed openly and honestly. This is also true for couples who are engaged and planning their wedding. When a couple becomes engaged, they are telling God and everyone that they are committed to each other, and this includes the financial aspect of their lives.

I have seen couples go into marriage without any idea of the financial situation that their future spouse may be carrying with them. Once you say "I do," you both take on each other's financial responsibility. I have also seen couples who keep separate savings and checking accounts, and I can tell you that these types of agreement never work out. This is especially true if you have a heavy burden of debt.

If you are trying to finance a marriage and rid yourself of debt at the same time, you will not make any headway on the debt. When you bring the finances of a husband and wife and put them on the table, you can make smarter decisions on what to do to get rid of debt and begin saving.

The other problem with separate accounts is that, as one person told me, "It is easier to leave the marriage if things get rough. I already have money if I have to move out and pay rent somewhere else." I believe this problem speaks for itself.

There should always be some money for giving to your local church. If you put God first in your finances—and everything else, for that matter—He will help you. This is especially true with your finances. Money can be a tricky subject as it is the one thing most people watch very carefully and are afraid to part with.

When Misty and I got married, we both brought a lot of debt into the marriage. She had student loans, and I had a huge credit card debt. Misty and I were living in California when we were first married. We started to attend church and give on a regular weekly basis. We found ourselves short of a great deal of money, but it was decided that we would give to church anyway and trust God to provide for what we needed.

At the last second, when we thought our financial situation was going to go very bad quickly, I went to the mailbox. In the mailbox was a check for what we needed, and five dollars extra. The strange thing about this check was it was for a life insurance policy I had cancelled many years before. I had moved three times since I had cancelled this policy, and the only way they could have found me was through God. This has happened on more than one occasion, and though we have a budget, we lean heavily on God to help us financially. We must do our part and give first to God out of our love for Him.

The question may come up about how much to give. I can tell you that 10 percent is a good place to start, but this is between you and God. In Mark 12:41–44 and Luke 21:1–4, when a poor widow walks into the temple to give, Jesus is in the temple watching people give their offerings, and when He sees what she has to offer, He calls His disciples over to teach them. Mark records this event in the following way:

"And He (Jesus) sat down opposite the treasury, and began observing how the people were putting money into the treasury; and many rich people were putting in large sums. A poor widow came and put in two small copper coins, which amount to a cent. Calling His disciples to Him, He said to them, 'Truly I say to you, this poor widow put in more than all the contributors to the treasury; for they all put in out of their surplus, but she, out of her poverty, put in all she owned, all she had to live on.'"

God wants you to give from your heart, and only you know what you should give.

I want to give a word of warning here. There are people who will teach you that if you give a certain amount of money to God that He will bless you with a larger sum of money. I will tell you that this type of teaching is dangerous, and I personally know of a couple of people who have given their life savings to some of these teachers and are now in financial ruin. You must use wisdom when giving.

There also needs to be a savings plan in place. As you look at the income that you and your spouse bring in to the marriage, it is a good idea to come up with some percentage that you both are comfortable with to save for the future. As you work on your budget, always make sure to input something for saving and emergencies.

There is a joy in giving to God, and the blessing you receive back is more than you can ever ask for. This is not necessarily monetary, but God's blessings can come in many forms. However, do not give to get, give because you love God. The verse in 2 Corinthians 9:6–7 says,

"Now this I say, he who sows sparingly will also reap sparingly, and he who sows bountifully will also reap bountifully. Each one must do just as he has purposed in his heart, not grudgingly or under compulsion, for God loves a cheerful giver."

Are you and your spouse cheerful givers? A cheerful giver will starve the Dragon of Money. There is nothing more than this dragon wants than to make sure you are struggling financially. Have open communication about money with your spouse, and the Dragon of Money will not be a problem for you.

Discussion Questions for the Dragon of Money

1. Do you and your spouse have a budget, and do you follow it?
2. Do you and your spouse have any debt that is interfering with your marriage?
3. Do you handle credit cards wisely?
4. Do you save each pay period?
5. Are you a cheerful giver?
6. What scriptures can the two of you use to defeat a Dragon of Money?

Notes

CHAPTER 14

The Dragon of Anger

"Be angry, and yet do not sin; do not let the sun go down on your anger, and do not give the devil an opportunity." (Ephesians 4:26–27)

I am fairly confident that at some time in our lives we have heard the comment "Don't go to bed angry." There is a lot of truth to that statement, especially in marriage.

This dragon is especially dangerous when it comes to the marriage covenant, and if one person goes to bed angry, the Dragon of Anger can easily take over and begin to work on both the husband and the wife.

Paul's warning in the above Scripture goes so far as to say that if you allow yourself to let the sun go down on your anger, the devil will then have an opportunity to "get involved" in your anger. What this means is that if Satan gets involved in your anger, your anger will control you, and that leads to sin.

There is a righteous anger, such as the anger Jesus experienced in John 2:13–16, but in many circumstances, anger leads to bigger problems. Anger can also be a sign of something deeper that has been going on for a while.

If the Dragon of Anger begins to rear is ugly head, it can get out of control quickly. When working with married couples, I have seen anger ignite in seconds to the point where everyone just needed to stop and take a few breaths before moving forward with the discussion.

The Dragon of Anger appears quickly and does not like going back to its lair. It enjoys causing havoc, and most of the time, we are very good at feeding it. Unfortunately, when you feed this dragon, it sticks around looking for more food. This dragon needs to be starved to death before it causes serious damage to the marriage.

With all this being said, eventually one of you will release a Dragon of Anger. This dragon originates from our sin nature and emotions combined. Everyone is created with emotions. The God whom we serve is an emotional God, and throughout the Bible, you will see a God who gets angry. However, He controls His anger and only allows Himself to be angry in a holy and righteous way.

Psalm 103:8–9 says, "The Lord is compassionate and gracious, slow to anger and abounding in loving kindness. He will not always strive with us, nor will He keep His anger forever." God forgives immediately when asked. He does not hold His anger over any of us as long as we ask for forgiveness. If we were to follow His example each time we begin to get angry with our spouse, we would slay the Dragon of Anger and the Dragon of Unforgiveness at the same time.

When we look at the way the Dragon of Anger can be released, it is important to understand that everyone is different, and because of these differences, people will get angry at different situations and circumstances. What upsets me may not upset you. It is just the way we are made, or it may be the way we were raised. If I grew up watching one of my parents get angry each time one of them did not want to wash a dish, there is a good chance that I will have the same reaction if my wife does not want to wash a dish.

Each of us must take into account what upsets our spouses, and we must be aware of what happens if we are to say or do something that upsets them. Some people will become very quiet and withdraw from the relationship; others will become quite angry and lose control of all their emotions. Understanding how your spouse handles anger is so very important. If your spouse is one who withdraws when angry, this could be misunderstood as a disinterest in you and your marriage covenant. If you know this is how they handle their emotion of anger, then you can handle it accordingly.

I am one who withdraws for a while to calm down and think through what had just happened. Misty knows that if something is said that upsets me I just need to walk away and process it. She knows this because I told her this is how I deal with certain situations and circumstances. She does the same, which makes it real interesting around the home if we both have something come up that we need to process before moving forward.

If your spouse is one who loses control of their emotions, there is a good chance they will respond with words that will be damaging. At this point, you will probably have a full-blown fight on your hands, and it will take a much-longer time to bring calmness to the situation.

You will also have to deal with the words that may have been spoken in anger. The person who handles anger this way is much more difficult to handle than one who withdraws. When a person gets so angry that they lose control, they will not be able to listen to reason. How many times have you heard someone say when they were around someone who was experiencing anger, "They were so crazy they did not listen to any thing I had to say!" People can get "anger deaf" or fly into a blind rage, and sometimes, you just have to ride it out with them.

With either of these types of people, the best thing you can do is tell them that you love them and you are there for them when they are ready to talk. The person who has lost control may be not listening, but they may hear you, and that may be enough to calm them down.

Here is another consideration. If your spouse is constantly getting angry, there is probably some deeper issue that needs to be dealt with. If there is a constant struggle with anger, there should be a discussion to discover the root cause. Most of the time, I have seen people sit down and talk, and something comes up in the discussion that the person with the anger issue never understood.

If after a few discussions nothing has been accomplished, you may need to seek professional counseling to help. This deeper issue could be a sin of some type. When people are living in sin, they usually get angry as the Holy Spirit is convicting them. It is true that you can ignore the Holy Spirit for a while, but I can tell you that He will eventually put enough pressure on you that you will start to show some cracks, and that is where the anger can come from.

If you are or your spouse is dealing with this type of anger, just go back to God and ask for forgiveness. You will also need to ask for forgiveness from your spouse.

Finally, I want to discuss the worst part of this dragon. The Dragon of Anger can be one of a physical nature. I want to say this is clearly as I can: no one has the right to lay a hand on another person in anger, ever! If you are in a situation where there is some form of a physical situation going on due to anger, get out *now*! This person who is physically attacking may be in that blind rage that I had mentioned earlier, and they may have lost control to the point where they need to release their anger in a physical way. They will react before they can think and act. Reaction in this situation almost always has a bad result. Never allow yourself to be in harm's way.

The Dragon of Anger is a dragon that can cause deep issues in the marriage covenant. The words that are spoken in anger are often difficult to deal with, and they can have long-lasting consequences.

If you are to hurt your spouse with words spoken in anger, you can expect your spouse to need some time to work through those feelings. You can ask for forgiveness, and it can, and should, be granted.

However, just because forgiveness is granted does not mean that the person who has been hurt will be over the emotion of the hurt. It sometimes takes time to heal from words. The old saying that sticks and stones will break my bones but words will never hurt me is far from the truth. I remember spoken words more than I remember any other type of hurt that I had received in anger from another person. I again ask you to please be patient with your spouse as they deal with the hurt that had been spoken.

Discussion Questions for the Dragon of Anger

1. Do you have an anger issue?
2. Do you withdraw or attack when angry?
3. Are you angry with your spouse now? Why?
4. Have you spoken with angry words to your spouse? Have you made it right with them?
5. Do you need to speak with a professional about your anger?
6. What scriptures can the two of you use to defeat a Dragon of Anger?

Notes

CHAPTER 15

The Dragon of Coveting

"You shall not covet your neighbor's house; you shall not covet your neighbor's wife or his male servant or his female servant or his ox or his donkey or anything that belongs to your neighbor." (Exodus 20:17)

Have you ever driven by your neighbor's house and seen that brand-new car in their driveway and thought how nice it would be to have one too? Have you thought that about other material things that someone you know has in his or her possession?

The Dragon of Coveting is a tricky one. This dragon, if released, can release many other dragons into the marriage covenant. The Dragons of Anger, Money, Sex, and Communication can all be set free to run rampant in a marriage if this dragon is not dealt with swiftly.

I want you to understand that this dragon goes beyond material things. The big problem comes into play when you start to desire another person, a certain employment, or something else that takes you away from focusing on God and your spouse.

The Dragon of Coveting is like the old saying about "playing with fire." Sure, it keeps you warm on a cold night, but it can also burn your house down if you are not careful. The smoke from a fire can suffocate you too. As dragons breathe fire, this analogy seems appropriate. So be careful what you desire in your heart.

When one begins to desire something to the point where they are thinking about it almost constantly, these thoughts will begin to take over. The danger here is that the thoughts will eventually lead to actions. Let's say a friend of yours has just purchased a brand-new sports car. You see this car on a daily basis, and all of a sudden, your thoughts take over and you start thinking about what it would be like to drive it. If you think on this long enough, the conversation may take place with your spouse about buying one. Even though you cannot afford it, you talk your spouse into buying one. Your car is very old, and you feel that you deserve a new car. You do not pray about buying it; you want it, and you want it soon. This car has now become an idol and is about to cause you problems.

Now that you have your shiny new car in your garage, the realization of the financial burden comes upon you. When this happens, you now have two dragons being released in your marriage. The Dragon of Money is now teaming up with the Dragon of Coveting. This is a dangerous partnership, and they will be looking for other dragons to join them. You may think that because you have talked this purchase over with your spouse that the Dragon of Communication will not be a problem.

Let me ask this: did you ask your spouse, or did you lovingly manipulate the conversation so that the purchase of the car sounded more like a need than a want? You may be questioning how that is even possible. Let me assure you, I have heard this more than once, and the spouse who is trying to convince the other about purchasing something is excellent at making their argument.

There are a couple of questions that should be asked about purchasing something that you would like, but first, ask yourself, "Is this a want or a need?" Second, if it is a need, can you afford it, or can you get by with a much-cheaper model so you do not get yourself in so much debt that it will take years to recover? Third, if it is a need and you can afford it, will there be any concerns in the marriage if you buy it?

An example I use is that about three years ago, I wanted to buy a motorcycle. I had one in my "youth," and the desire for one was taking over some of my thoughts on a regular basis. This was especially true on one of those eighty-degree days when it was the perfect day for motorcycle riding.

Misty and I talked about it, and she said I could buy one if I really wanted it. Now, some of you men are raising your fist in the air and screaming, "Yes, that's awesome! What a great wife you have!" Yes, it is true I have a great wife—so do you, by the way—but there is something that you need to know that made the decision a little more difficult.

Years ago, Misty was dating a young man who was riding an ATV without a helmet, and he crashed. He suffered some permanent disabilities, and it was very difficult for Misty to deal with. If I had purchased that motorcycle, do you think that Misty would be concerned about me every time I started it and drove off? The answer is absolutely. I was not willing to put her in a situation where she would have a concern every time I left the house on two wheels.

Am I saying that motorcycles are dangerous? No, I am saying that my wife saw a dear friend of hers have his life changed forever because of a foolish decision not to wear a helmet. Now, I would wear a helmet, and I am a very careful rider, but I was not willing to put her through that.

So I just took my thoughts off the motorcycle, and eventually, the strong desire went away. Do I still want a motorcycle? Yes, but I am not making it the idol that it was becoming. I am just not willing to put Misty through wondering if I am going to be hurt. This is one of those Dragons of Uncertainty that I am unwilling to release into our marriage.

I would like to say that just because you cannot afford to buy something now does not mean you will not be in a position to buy it later. When I was seventeen years old, I saw a Trans Am in the local Pontiac dealership. It was gold, and had the phoenix on the hood. It also had the T-top that was so prevalent back then.

My dad and I went down to the dealership, and he knew most of the people who worked there and introduced me to one of the salesmen. This salesman asked me if I wanted to test-drive the car, and I just about ran him over running toward the car. I must tell you that not many cars have had the effect that driving that car had on me. It was fast—really fast—and it was comfortable to drive.

Then he told me the price.

I must have gotten that look on my face that told him I was just a poor seventeen-year-old, and then he said this to me, "You have your whole life ahead of you to buy a car like this."

Now it is true that none of us know how long we will be on this earth, and it is also true that Pontiac is out of business and I will never be able to buy a car like that, but what he said made sense to me. Sometimes we have to wait a while to get what we would like to have.

The Dragon of Covetousness that I truly want to address is the one that can be the most dangerous. This is the emotional part of this dragon. This is the one where you see a person and desire them. It may be a coworker, the person at the grocery store, or maybe even a past romantic relationship where the person has shown up in your life.

I want to say this as gently as I can: you need to run away from this person and run quick! Galatians 5:16–17 says, "But I say, walk by the Spirit, and you will not carry out the desire of the flesh. For the flesh sets its desire against the Spirit, and the Spirit against the flesh; for these are in opposition to one another, so that you may not do the things that you please."

We must rely on the power of the Holy Spirit to help us deal with temptations that can lead to sin. If we are to covet that person, we are asking for those thoughts to turn to actions, and those actions will lead to this dragon running into your marriage and causing great harm or, in some severe cases, irreparable damage.

The emotional part of this dragon may sound dangerous, and it is. However, this dragon is also easily defeated. If you do not feed this dragon with sinful thoughts, he will starve. This may sound easy, and to be honest, some people will struggle with this.

The best thing I can tell you is make sure your heart and thoughts are on Jesus and your spouse. To do this, is all you need to do is to be in prayer and ask God how to bring the desire you had for your spouse back to you and to remove the desire that you may have for another. God may allow a time of testing in this, but I can tell you that once you get through this type of test, your marriage will be stronger than ever.

The way to slay this dragon sounds simple. To slay this dragon, you just need to change your thoughts. For example, if I started talking about a hot fudge sundae and was talking about the ice cream, the hot fudge sauce, the whipped cream, and a cherry on top, some of you may think about that enough to want to go get one to eat.

Now, here is the question: what were you thinking about before you started to read about that sundae? You were probably thinking of something else. That is how easy and quickly thoughts can change.

Paul tells us in Philippians 4:8 what to do with our thoughts: "Finally, brethren, whatever is true, whatever is honorable, whatever is right, whatever is pure, whatever is lovely, whatever is of good repute, if there is any excellence and if anything worthy of praise, dwell on these things."

Please dwell on the things that God would dwell on, and this dragon will fly away from you and your marriage.

Discussion Questions for the Dragon of Coveting

1. Do you struggle with coveting what others have? Why do you think this is?
2. Are you content with what God has given you? Why or why not?
3. Have you put yourself or your family in a financial concern because of purchases that have been made that were not needs? Do you have a plan to get out of this debt? What is that plan?
4. Do you have thoughts desiring another who is not your spouse? How are you correcting this?
5. Have you allowed any other dragons to creep in your marriage while dealing with coveting? Which ones?
6. What scriptures can the two of you use to defeat a Dragon of Coveting?

Notes

CHAPTER 16

The Dragon of Submission

"Wives, be subject to your own husbands, as to the Lord. For the husband is the head of the wife, as Christ also is the head of the church, He Himself being the Savior of the body. But as the church is subject to Christ, so also the wives ought to be to their husbands in everything. Husbands, love your wives, just as Christ also loved the church and gave Himself up for her, so that He might sanctify her, having cleansed her by the washing of water with the word, that He might present to Himself the church in all her glory, having no spot or wrinkle or any such thing; but that she would be holy and blameless. So husbands ought also to love their own wives as their own bodies. He who loves his own wife loves himself; for no one ever hated his own flesh, but nourishes and cherishes it, just as Christ also does the church, because we are members of His body." (Ephesians 5:22–30)

If you made it past the Scripture and have begun reading this section, know I am grateful that you are giving me a chance to explain this dragon. If you are a male and are taking this book and pointing this Scripture out to your wife, telling her that she needs to submit to you because God says so, you may end up wearing this book. If you are a female who read the Scripture above and have thrown the book across the room or at your finger-pointing husband, I am glad that you have picked this book back up and kept reading.

This dragon lives on the misunderstanding of what it means to submit. He thrives on it. I have seen men throw this Scripture around like they wrote it, and I have seen women roll their eyes and say, "I will never submit to any man, ever!" All this is because the word *submission* is being misunderstood.

First, let me say that submission is for both men and women. Ephesians 5:21 says, "And be subject to one another in the fear of Christ." Most people skip that Scripture. When you put it all together, one can see that submission to God first and then each other is what should be done.

When a husband submits to God in all that he is doing, then the wife should have no problem submitting to her husband. It is important to know that this passage of Scripture does not give the husband the right to become a dictator. The earthly ministry of Jesus never once saw Jesus abuse His authority that was given to Him by God.

Men, you are the spiritual leaders of the home. God has given that authority to you. Do not ever abuse that authority. Paul's words tell husbands to love their wives as themselves. Husbands, how do you want your wife to treat you? Do you want her to push you around, nagging you all day long? Probably not. Your wife does not want you to go around taking advantage of Paul's words any more than God does.

Wives, this passage tells you to submit to your husband. Please understand that this is not a bad thing. Think of it like this: if your husband is following God's lead by submitting to Him, why would you not want to follow your husband? The one word I have heard from women who submit to godly men would be *freeing*. I have heard many Christian women use that term. You become free as you follow God's direction.

This does not mean you sit there and say nothing. It means that you give input when you are having a discussion and you ask questions if there is a concern. Just as this Scripture does not give the husband the right to be a dictator, so does it not mean you are to be a doormat.

According to Romans 8:17, all Christians—men and women—are joint heirs with Christ. There is equality, yet there is a chain of command that God has put in place for reasons He alone knows. When one reads the account of Creation and the order He created everything, one sees that God created man first and then woman. Again, there is nothing wrong with the order that He created; He is an orderly God, and He wanted things a certain way.

Along with the Fall in the book of Genesis comes a curse that every woman has to deal with. In Genesis 3:16, it says, "Yet your desire will be for your husband, and he shall rule over you." Do not get excited about the word *rule*. Scripture always supports Scripture, so looking at Ephesians 5:23, you will see that "the husband is the head of the wife as Christ also is the head of the church." Christ rules the husband, as a husband rules over the wife. We should stop looking at submission in a negative light and submit to God who can change our lives and strengthen our marriages.

The best way to look at submission is to look at the Trinity. Here you have God the Father, God the Son, and God the Holy Spirit all working together in submission.

In the Bible, do you ever see any member of the Trinity arguing about who is in charge? No! There is a submission and a peace within the Trinity when they work together and submit to each other. It is a beautiful demonstration of what a marriage should look like.

Is there ever a time a husband or wife should not submit to their spouse? The answer is yes. If the husband or wife is acting in an unbiblical manner or not following Scripture, the spouse needs to lovingly confront their husband or wife and explain that there are some things that they cannot do because of biblical commands.

An extreme example of this would be to steal. A not-so-extreme example would be to break the speed limit because you are running late for an event. Some of you are reading this and wondering how can breaking the speed limit be against biblical standards. Romans 13:1 says that we must "be in subjection to the governing authorities." As those governing authorities have set the speed limit, so must we follow those rules. God is the ultimate authority, and even though not all men will follow God's principles, He still has people in certain positions to make those rules.

Another way to look at this dragon would be to think about how many times you have come across a company or business that has so many people leading it that no one gets anything accomplished. There are so many people in charge that there is no one submitting to another. Everyone has their own agenda, and each person wants what they want.

In a marriage, this cannot work. If a husband or wife only thinks about what they want out of the marriage, no growth can occur. Selfishness stops growth dead in its tracks.

What should submission look like to a married couple? Let's say there is a decision that needs to be made. If both husband and wife take their concern to God in prayer, they should come up with the same answer. If they both come up with a different response, here is where submission becomes interesting.

Let's say this is a financial decision that needs to be made. There is a need for new furniture, and you are both not sure that this is the time to buy. When in prayer one person believes that God wants them to wait, the other believes God is saying now is the time to buy.

Who is right in this situation? God will not tell the husband or wife one thing and tell the other something completely opposite. Only one can be correct. It could be that one person is imposing their own will into the prayer so that they can get new furniture.

Whatever the reason, this could cause the Dragon of Submission to be released. If the husband is imposing his will and wants the new furniture and the wife believes now is not the time, the final decision goes to the husband.

As difficult as it is for the women to be reading this, it is the way God has set things up. When the husband purchases the furniture and things do not work out as well, it is important for the wife to just not say anything. The words "I told you so" never work out well here. When those words are spoken, the Dragon of Submission is released and havoc is brought into the marriage.

We are all going to make an error in judgment at one time or another, and it is important to love the one who has made the error. If you start berating your spouse when they make an error, the Dragon of Submission will be released and things will go bad quickly. This can also release the Dragon of Unforgiveness and the Dragon of Anger, as you will probably speak harshly to the spouse who made the error. Be ready to forgive and move on.

The Dragon of Submission can be tricky. As previously stated, this dragon lives off the misunderstanding of the term. However, once this dragon is defeated, the marriage will grow exponentially and the husband and wife will have a strong, godly marriage.

Discussion Questions for the Dragon of Submission

1. Do you struggle with submitting to God?
2. Husbands, are you a dictator, or do you look to your wife for input on decisions?

3.   Wives, do you fight against submitting to your husband?
4.   Husbands and wives, do you submit to each other?
5.   What scriptures can the two of you use to defeat a Dragon
     of Submission?

Notes

CHAPTER 17

The Dragon of Conflict

"A gentle answer turns away wrath, but a harsh word stirs up anger." (Proverbs 15:1)

Conflict is inevitable. I have often said anytime there is more than one person in a room there will be a difference of opinion, and that can lead to a conflict of some nature. This does not necessarily mean that a relationship will be destroyed, but it means that one needs to be careful with what they say and how they say it.

Conflicts will arise in marriage; as men and women see things differently, there are going to be differences of opinions. There have been times when I have said something so clearly that there is no doubt with what I have said—at least no doubt in my mind. When Misty hears it, she looks at me kind of funny and tells me she has no idea what I am talking about. How is this possible? I just said it clear as day, and you are telling me that you do not understand?

When the Dragon of Conflict arises, it is important to lovingly speak your mind without going on the defensive right away. We must be careful not only with the way we say something but also in the body language that we use. If we take a defensive stance, our spouse will immediately notice that we are attacking and not discussing. When this happens, escalation can follow shortly after unless something is done quickly to diffuse the situation. At this point, the Dragon of Conflict begins his attack.

Here is a question I want to ask you before moving forward: "Would you rather be right or reconciled?" It is a question I use on a regular basis. If there is a discussion happening that you feel is leading to a conflict, it is fine to stop and ask yourself this question. This does not mean you are not allowed to voice your opinion; it just means that you want to have a solution to the discussion that does not lead to an argument that releases the Dragon of Conflict and the discussion now gets out of control.

One of the ways to handle this is to communicate your feelings and thoughts to your spouse about how you act in a conflict. An example is I am one who needs to retreat to work through my thoughts and emotions. I also do not want to say something that would release a dragon. Retreating is not a bad thing in itself, but it caused us some issues when I was first married. If Misty and I had a disagreement, I would get very quiet and retreat to another room. Misty thought I wanted to leave the marriage, but what I was doing was trying to keep my head straight and my emotions in check. That's just the way I am, and once I told her this, she understood.

It was a simple conversation, and all I had to tell her was that I needed a little time to work through the emotions and the discussion, and that I just needed to go to another room to figure it out. It changed the way we looked at conflict.

Let me give you a warning here: never leave the house and drive away. Tell your spouse you need to clear your head and walk to another room or sit in silence while you work through everything. In the decade that I have led a marriage group, I can tell you that I have seen people leave their homes during a conflict more than they should have. They start to use leaving as a crutch, and they just get up and go at the slightest disagreement.

The great thing about me communicating to Misty that I needed some space is that when we have a disagreement now, I do not leave. I sit with her as I work through the problem. Something changed in me once I communicated this personality trait. I killed the Dragon of Conflict and moved on to a stronger marriage.

Misty did the same for me. She either retreats or questions me, so I never know which way she is going to deal with this dragon. However, she now tells me which way she is going to deal with our conflict, and I can then address whatever concerns she may have, knowing how she handles the particular conflict we are having. It is all about communicating how you handle conflict to your spouse. Once they know how you handle conflict, they will be able to work through the conflict with you.

During His earthly ministry, Jesus handled conflict on a regular basis with the religious leaders of the day. In some cases, He caused the conflict because He made them think, and when He spoke, it went against everything these men had been taught. The reason so much conflict came about from these conversations was that they did not believe Jesus was who He said He was. He also handled them with tough love. Though they did not want to hear what He had to say, He spoke the truth.

The same goes in our marriages. When we speak truth—and this truth must be spoken with love—our spouse may not like what we have to say. What we say will be something that, once worked through, will give us a stronger marriage. It is imperative that once we hear the truth that we should not react to what we have just heard. No one likes hearing that we have hurt our spouse, but if we have hurt them, we should listen to what we have done and then work on correcting the situation together.

I cannot emphasize how important it is to work together to solve a conflict. One of the better ways to approach this would be if you were to go your spouse and let them know there is an issue that is bothering you and you would like to come up with a plan to attack it together. This takes a lot of the pressure off your spouse, and they will not feel that you are just blaming them for something that has happened, or that is occurring.

When two attack this dragon together, it will be slain quickly. In the book of Ecclesiastes, in verses 4:9–12, we are given a great example of two working together:

> *"Two are better than one because they have a good*
> *return for their labor. For if either of them falls,*
> *the one will lift up his companion. But woe to the*
> *one who falls when there is not another to lift him*
> *up. Furthermore, if two lie down together they*
> *keep warm, but how can one be warm alone? And*
> *if one can overpower him who is alone, two can*
> *resist him. A cord of three strands is not quickly*
> *torn apart."*

If God, you, and your spouse work together to solve a conflict, how much better will that be? This is one of those dragons that will need to be defeated with two working together. If this dragon is to succeed at his mission, he will divide you and your spouse and then attack you separately. With division comes weakness. There is something to be said about strength in numbers, even if it is only two of you. As you bring God into the battle, the victory will be swift.

Discussion Questions for the Dragon of Conflict

1. Are you currently dealing with a conflict in your marriage?
2. Are you someone who retreats or attacks when confronted with a conflict?

3. How have you dealt with conflict in the past?
4. How will you deal with conflict in the future?
5. How do you handle constructive criticism?
6. What scriptures can the two of you use to defeat a Dragon of Conflict?

Notes

CHAPTER 18

The Dragon of Technology

"You shall have no other gods before Me." (Exodus 20:3)

You may think that this chapter's Scripture has nothing to do with the topic, but I would have to disagree. We have created so many gods that keep us busy and occupied that we are losing the ability to interact socially.

Look around you the next time you are in a public place, and watch how people interact with each other and how they interact with the technology they are using. We are so connected with our technology that we are losing our ability to communicate with each other. Cell phones, tablets, computers, and a host of other electronic devices keep us sidetracked and distracted. Whether or not we want to hear it, we have made technology a god, and we worship it almost constantly.

Now that I have stepped on some of your toes, I would like to say that using technology for the way it was intended is not a bad thing. I personally use a cell phone, and it has come in handy on many occasions. However, if I were to "live" on the phone and ignore my wife, problems would quickly arise.

The Dragon of Technology is a sneaky dragon and will creep up on you, slithering low on the ground so no one can see him.

I am a little bit of a weather geek. I am amazed at how God has created the weather. With this being said, I have a couple of weather apps on my phone. I have been known to watch the radar for incoming rain or snow. Every once in a while, I find myself watching the radar app when I know there are approaching storms.

I knew there was a potential problem a few years ago when I was at dinner and pulled out my phone to watch the approaching front of weather. Misty pointed out to me that we were out at dinner and my phone should not even be out of my pocket. Point well taken.

About a year after this incident, I took Misty to a water park for her birthday. We left the phones locked in the car, and it was probably the most freeing day I have had in a long time. Being in ministry, I try to be available for people as much as possible, but I need to be available for Misty too. It is a difficult balance to find for pastors and people in ministry. Misty also counsels people, and she gets the occasional phone call from someone. I have no problem when she has to help someone. She has no problem when I need to help either, but we need to have a balance so that our marriage is not affected.

You may need to find a balance with your technology. If so, may I please offer you a few suggestions to help you? If you are very attached to some form of technology, this may not be easy at first, but know this dragon can be tamed so that the technology becomes a tool and not a possible hindrance.

Let me just say before I go any further that there are some occupations that need their cell phones due to the nature of their work. A doctor, for example, needs to be reached if they are on call. However, let me say this: a doctor needs to receive calls on their phone, and they do not need to be watching the weather radar when they are out with their husband or wife. There is a huge difference in needing their phone and wanting their phone for a certain app.

First, start by putting your phone away. Sounds easy enough, right? It may not be. If you have created a habit of grabbing your phone and looking at it, your phone has now become an extension of your body. This "extension" is going to seem very abnormal if you do not have it in your hand. It will take time, and your spouse may need to help you break this habit.

I promise nothing horrible will happen to you if you do not use your phone for a couple of hours while you are spending some time with your spouse. Now, something bad may happen if you do not put the phone away, especially if your spouse is sitting there looking at you, wanting to have a conversation.

If your life or someone else's life does not depend on it, leave the phone in the car while you watch a movie or have dinner. You can actually leave your phone off or in another room even if you are at home! I am really stepping on toes now, aren't I? That is not my intent. My intent is to make sure that your marriage is protected from the Dragon of Technology.

Second, if the Internet is a problem for you, you can come up with a schedule to turn on your computer to check e-mails or social media. Put an accountability plan in place by checking e-mails or social media with your spouse. When you're done, you can shut down the computer and spend some time talking about some of the things you have just read on social media.

Third, as habits take some time to break, do not be concerned if you cannot let go of that electronic device quickly. It takes about twenty-one days to make or break a habit. Do not push so hard that you awaken another dragon. Be patient with yourself and your spouse, and take it to God in prayer. Psalm 46:1 says, "God is our strength, a very present help in trouble."

If you are struggling, know our Father in heaven will be there to help you through your struggle. He loved you enough to send His one and only Son to die for all of us; I can promise you that He loves you enough to help you. All you need to do is ask.

Technology in itself is not bad. We actually need technology. It is a tool that, if used properly, can make our lives easier. If abused, it can make our lives more difficult. When you put any piece of technology above God or your spouse, you have now made that electronic device an idol. Those may be harsh words, but they are truth. As we are surrounded by technology, we need to be aware of when this particular dragon awakens.

We have technology in our hands, homes, cars, and workplaces. Everywhere we look, we see there is some button to push or some flashing light blasting us in our faces. It is here to stay, but that does not mean that it has to affect us and our marriages in a negative way. We alone are responsible for the way we handle our technology and how we use it. If we allow it to overtake us, it is no longer a tool. If we use it to benefit our lives, it is a tool. Tools are used to better our lives and make them easier. Anything that causes problems in our lives is a dragon.

There is another attack that the Dragon of Technology uses, and that attack is toward our children. The problem with this particular attack is that the parents—you reading this book, possibly—are the ones who release dragons to attack them. I have seen parents control their children's technology use very well. I have also seen the opposite.

Again, technology is a tool that should be used wisely with parental guidance. There are young children using technology for school. This is a great idea. It is when the child uses the technology for hours upon hours that a dragon may be released. A child will also do what they see the parents do, so it is important that technology use is controlled across the board in the family.

If you have a situation where the Dragon of Technology has been released toward your children, know it is important for both parents to come together, agree on what to do, and then do it. If you both feel that the technology needs to be removed from your child for a time, then you do this together, explaining why it is being taken away.

Word of warning: never threaten a child with you taking away their technology and not doing it. That child will rule over you for a long time if this happens. This could also release a Dragon of Children that you do not want to deal with. Children are much more cunning than we give them credit for, and they know how to "work the system" when it comes to dealing with their parents. Always show unity when dealing with children. They need to know and see that Dad and Mom are working together.

Slaying this dragon can be very difficult. Our lives are so entrenched in technology that it has become part of us. However, defeating this dragon is like any other. Once you recognize this dragon, you must come up with a game plan with your spouse to defeat it.

Discussion Questions for the Dragon of Technology

1. Do you spend more time with an electronic device than you do with God?
2. Do you spend more time with an electronic device than you do with your spouse?
3. Have you asked God to help you break away from using some of your technology?
4. Have you asked your spouse to help you with cutting back on using technology?
5. Have you and your spouse ever discussed something you have read on social media? Are you willing to do this starting today?

6. Do you think that technology has become too common-place today?
7. How would you react if someone took your technology away for one week? One month? One year?
8. If you have children, do you think that they spend too much time using some form of technology? Do you and your spouse have a plan to deal with this?
9. What scriptures can the two of you use to defeat a Dragon of Technology?

Notes

CHAPTER 19

The Dragon of Time

"Now as they were traveling along, He entered a village; and a woman named Martha welcomed Him into her home. She had a sister called Mary, who was seated at the Lord's feet, listening to His word. But Martha was distracted with all her preparations; and she came up to Him and said, 'Lord, do You not care that my sister has left me to do all the serving alone? Then tell her to help me.' But the Lord answered and said to her, 'Martha, Martha, you are worried and bothered about so many things; but only one thing is necessary, for Mary has chosen the good part, which shall not be taken away from her.'" (Luke 10:38–42)

Time. There seems to never be enough of it, or could it be that we are just not prioritizing our lives properly? We serve an eternal God. One who has no watches, clocks, or calendars. A God who has given us time as a gift. Twenty-four hours a day, seven days a week, 365 days a year. This gift of time needs to be used wisely, or the Dragon of Time will enter our lives and distract us from what is important.

I have heard many couples complain about how much they are running around for themselves or with their children and going to all types of events. Youth events at church, sporting events, music lessons, school trips, movies, amusement parks, and a host of other "things to do," and they barely have time for their spouse.

When you read this list, which one stands out as the most important to you? Most important to your spouse? Which one do you believe your child would choose to be their choice? Is your choice one that is even on this short list? Some of you may be having some trouble deciding what you would choose.

Martha and Mary are two women who want to please Jesus, but it was Mary who was listening to what Jesus had to say. Martha was complaining that Mary was not helping. She became so frustrated that she actually asked Jesus to tell her sister to get up and help! That was bold. Martha was so distracted that she was missing what Jesus had to say.

See where being busy gets us? We get so busy that we will miss Jesus and what He wants us to do, or tell us. Though it is important to make sure that we are listening and serving our spouses, it is also important to make sure we make time for God first. Simply put, if we spend time with God first, the rest of our day will be easier.

I always start my day with prayer before my feet hit the floor. If I miss this time of prayer, my day does not go so well.

If the Dragon of Time is released, there will be so much craziness during your day you may not be able to keep a schedule at all. This dragon is one who is quiet and methodical. He will keep you so busy and will whisper in your ear that you need to keep doing everything you can do. The busier you are, the more "exciting" your life will be. Though it is true that your life will be exciting, it may cost you.

Jesus tells Martha that her sister has chosen the good part—listening to Him—and that He is telling her to rethink what is important. I will do the same. Take the words of Jesus Christ, and try to figure out what is most important in your life. You can write it down if you need to, but take a look at your schedule. If you find that you are so busy, then the Dragon of Time may be attacking your marriage.

The only way to have a strong relationship is to spend time with the person you want to get to know better. If the Dragon of Time is interfering with this, a chasm will form in the relationship that you are developing. This developing relationship should always be with God first and your spouse second.

One thing I have always told Misty is that she will always be second to God. There is nothing wrong with this thought at all. It is my responsibility to make her feel like she is number one, but she will never be as important as God is. Some of you may think there is nothing about this thought process that is good. I can tell you that if you put God first, then the rest of your schedule will fall into place. This includes the time you spend with your spouse.

Be careful with this dragon. He is one who will make you believe that you have all the time in the world to do what you need to for your marriage. By the time you realize that you have been too busy, your spouse may be heading out the door.

This dragon likes to use work as one of its more popular attacks. This dragon will direct you to work more hours to make your life more "comfortable" because you will have the money to buy the things to make your life easy. Let me say this to you: life is never easy. It is hard. Buying material things will not make your life easy; it may make it easier, but not easy.

As human creations, we want our lives to be easy, but God does not promise that. Jesus makes it very clear in John 16:33 what our lives will be like: "These things I have spoken to you, so that in Me you may have peace. In the world you will have tribulation, but take courage; I have overcome the world."

The only way to make life peaceful would be through Jesus Christ. Please note that Jesus says nothing about life being easy. He actually says the opposite. You can have peace through your trials, and that peace will come through a personal relationship with Jesus Christ. Do not think for a moment that buying that new thing will bring you peace; it will not.

Another way this dragon attacks is after another dragon has already begun its attack. When a dragon attacks, this one will just tell you that you do not have to rush into deal with the problem. This will allow the problem to grow into something that may not be able to be contained quickly. He will whisper in your ear that you both just need time to deal with whatever situation has arisen.

Now it may be true that there is a cooling-down period needed, but that does not mean you just ignore the attacking dragon and allow a lot of time to pass before dealing with the issue. Think of it like this: when a dragon attacks the villagers, it comes in and breathes fire. If this dragon is attacking and it is setting fire to your marriage, the fire needs to be dealt with in the beginning, when the fire is at a point where it is easiest to contain. If you wait to put the fire out, it will be much harder to extinguish. You need to stop any attacking dragon quickly. There is never a "waiting period" to slay a marriage dragon.

I would like to mention one other way this dragon will attack. I believe our enemy uses this dragon for times we should be evangelizing. This dragon will tell you that you do not have to evangelize today because you will have plenty of time tomorrow or the next day.

We have no idea when Jesus will return. He could come back as you are reading this book. No one knows. We need to treat each day as though Jesus is coming back at this very moment in time to introduce those people whom God puts in our lives to Jesus Christ. Time is a precious gift from God that we need to use wisely.

Discussion Questions for the Dragon of Time

1. When you look at your daily, weekly, and monthly schedule, what do you see is the majority of your time spent on?
2. Do you think you spend enough time with God each day?
3. Do you think you spend enough time with your spouse each day?
4. Do you spend more time at work than with your spouse?
5. Do you spend a lot of time taking your children to all kinds of events?
6. What would you change in your daily schedule right now?
7. Do you buy into the lie that we will always have tomorrow to evangelize?
8. What scriptures can the two of you use to defeat a Dragon of Time?

Notes

CHAPTER 20

The Dragon of Divorce

"So they are no longer two, but one flesh. What therefore God has joined together, let no man separate." (Matthew 19:6)

The Dragon of Divorce is a nasty beast. This dragon comes in like a storm and does as much damage as it can, and it will leave behind it a trail of destruction that can reach for generations. It can either move slowly over a great deal of time or move swiftly, catching everyone off guard and unprepared for its attack on a marriage. It is a dragon to avoid at all costs.

Now, with that being said, it is important to understand that if you are in an abusive relationship, where there are serious issues, you may need to leave so no one gets hurt. I have already addressed that there is never a reason to put a hand on someone else in anger. This is unacceptable to God. We are all made in His image, and we are to treat each other with love and respect. We must see each other by looking at each other through God's eyes.

If we acted this way, the world would be a much better, and much different, place. However, if the spouse who is being abused leaves, restoration and reconciliation should be seriously considered.

The abusing spouse needs help, and getting that person help should be a priority so that they do not hurt themselves or another.

I am a strong believer that all marriage problems can be fixed. If a husband and wife are willing to honor the marriage covenant and do some work, the marriage can be saved. This will take patience, love, kindness, and dependence on God. The marriage may also need some type of mediator to help guide them through the restoration process.

I have seen marriages on the brink of divorce come back stronger after the husband and wife worked through all their issues and kept their focus on God, each other, and the marriage covenant. Unfortunately, there are the other couples who just refuse to do what they should, and the marriage ends.

One of the main reasons marriages end today would be selfishness. This is just an observation, but the world tells everyone that they need to be happy every second of every day, and when a couple hits a "speed bump," they would rather go find someone who makes them happy instead of working on the marriage they are already in.

Here is the problem with this type of thinking: they will eventually hit a speed bump with the new person, and what do you think happens when this occurs? They move on to the next person, and the same cycle repeats itself.

There are going to be struggles in a marriage. There are two people with different backgrounds and thoughts coming together. Even though you may have dated for a while, nothing quite prepares you for the moment when you move in together after the marriage ceremony. All of a sudden, there is another human being around you most of the time. You have to share every part of your life with this person, and people who have lived alone for a long time may struggle with this.

I was forty years old when I got married. I had lived alone for many years, and it was a struggle for me to share "my space" with anyone. Eventually, I worked through it, and now it feels strange when Misty has to go on a business trip and is not here at the house.

My point is that you can adjust. The excuse "I just cannot live with that person" is not true. You are choosing *not* to want to live with that person. To leave is a choice, and if you decide to leave, you are being selfish and not thinking about the devastation you are doing to another person. More importantly, you will be losing your testimony and God will not be honored.

Some of you are becoming frustrated with me right now as you read this. You are probably thinking that I have no idea what you are going through with your husband or wife. You are correct, I do not. But I do know that I have seen much in the past decade and almost all the divorces have one thing in common: they get a thought in their head of "I am not happy, so I am going to go somewhere else and be with someone who makes me happy."

Then they find themselves alone and run to the first person who will date them. They rush into their second, or third, marriage, and eventually, the same feelings come back, and they take off again. If this cycle is not addressed and dealt with, it will continue to haunt them. Ironically, the happiness they are looking for will never be had, and getting a divorce will only lead to more unhappiness.

We must be careful of our thoughts. If we are to believe the world's lies that we are supposed to be happy all the time, we are in for a rude awakening. We are told in Matthew 6:34 that we should "not worry about tomorrow; for tomorrow will care for itself. Each day has enough trouble of its own."

Sounds like Jesus knew what life would be like for us. We cannot always be happy, but according to Romans 15:13, we can have more than happiness: "Now may the God of hope fill you with joy and peace in believing, so that you will abound in hope by the power of the Holy Spirit." We can have joy, peace, and hope, but we must do so by the power of the Holy Spirit. That same power of the Holy

Spirit can move the mountains in your marriage and give new life to it.

Some of you reading this book may be married to someone who does not have a relationship with Jesus Christ. What do you do then? How do you find joy and peace in a home with someone who does not know Jesus Christ and may not want to? Is there a way to find and have peace in this situation? The answer is yes. It may not be easy, but if Scripture is followed, one can have a home that honors and glorifies God.

First, one needs to look at whether or not being married to an unsaved spouse is reason for divorce. The answer is not always simple, but it is biblical. The verse in 1 Corinthians 7:13 says, "And a woman who has an unbelieving husband, and he consents to live with her, she must not send her husband away." This refers to the spouse who comes to a personal relationship with Jesus Christ after the marriage. By application, this goes for either spouse.

Paul then moves on to this verse: "Yet if the unbelieving one leaves, let him leave; the brother or the sister is not under bondage in such cases, but God has called us to peace." This does not mean that the believer should not do anything to help the marriage stay together. In fact, every effort should be taken to save the marriage as the unbelieving spouse may come to know Jesus Christ through the one who believes.

The verse in 1 Peter 3:1–2 says, "In the same way, you wives, be submissive to your own husbands so that even if any of them are disobedient to the word, they may be won without a word by the behavior of their wives, as they observe your chaste and respect-ful behavior." So what does this mean? It means that actions speak louder than words. If you are a husband or a wife who is married to an unbeliever, you will be the godly man or woman whom you are supposed to be and act accordingly. If you act biblically, you may win the unbelieving spouse to Jesus Christ.

I have known couples who have had one spouse pray and act respectfully toward the unbelieving spouse and that spouse has come to a relationship with Jesus Christ. It works, because God says so! How exciting would it be to see your unbelieving spouse come to a personal relationship with Jesus Christ? All this can be done by your actions, and then the Holy Spirit moves that spouse toward Jesus Christ. This alone should be enough reason to not divorce your spouse. Honoring God is always the priority in a marriage covenant.

We have looked at one biblical reason for divorce, the unsaved spouse who wants to leave. We now need to look at another biblical reason, and that is the reason of sexual immorality. The world calls this an extramarital affair. God calls it sin. If we call some of our actions what God calls those decisions, then we may not act so sinful as often as we do.

Sexual immorality is mentioned a few times in the Bible when talking about marriage. In Matthew 5:32 and Matthew 19:9, Jesus tells His audience that the only reason to divorce is due to sexual unfaithfulness.

Summarizing, the two reasons for divorce would be the following: abandonment from an unsaved spouse and sexual immorality by a spouse. Again, it is important to remember that reconciliation and restoration are always the preference to God.

If you are in one of these categories, it is important to understand that reconciliation and restoration is always God's preference. You may be separated and working on your marriage, or you may have already started your divorce and the Holy Spirit is placing on your heart that you should not give up. Always follow God's leading. Do not listen to your friends, family, coworkers, or anyone else.

If God tells you to stay the course and work on something, you do that. You may be working on your marriage, and God seems distant and quiet. In my experience, it is in those quiet times when God is ready to do something big. Be patient, and wait to see what He will do. It may not be easy, but allow God to glorify Himself through your struggles, and when you get through and your marriage is better than ever, you will be glad you stayed the course.

God wants you to be successful through your struggles and not give up. I have seen people give up too soon, and I have also seen people divorce just because they wanted to be happy and thinking that by divorcing their husband or wife, that happiness they were searching for would come their way. They were wrong, very wrong, and they ended up in a relationship that was so destructive that it caused even more serious issues in their lives than if they had stayed with the original marriage.

There is also the person who continues to go from one relationship to another, never being satisfied with the person who they are with. Remember the toothpaste tube earlier in this book? Again, be careful of the toothpaste-tube syndrome. It may just be that the person who is complaining about where the tube is being squeezed is the person who needs to deal with some problem in their past before they can move forward in any relationship.

There are other thoughts on divorce, and we must be careful with how we look at things like gambling, pornography, excessive drinking, etc. Some believe that some of these things can take the place of the spouse and, by doing so, is a reason for divorce.

The best thing I can tell you is that if the Bible is silent on it, we should be also. Jesus is very specific in what He talks about, and we should always follow His teachings. Be very careful when you start talking about divorce because it is something that you want, and you are forcing your thoughts and feelings into a situation. God is, and has, the final word. We do not.

Discussion Questions for the Dragon of Divorce

1. Do you know anyone who has been divorced?
2. Do you believe that this divorce was based on Scripture, or do you believe that it was a "worldly" divorce?
3. Are you struggling with whether or not you should get a divorce, and do you have a biblical reason for divorcing your spouse?
4. Have you bought into the lie of the world that you need to be happy all the time and that includes your marriage?
5. If you are considering a divorce, are you willing to go get professional help before moving forward with it?
6. If you have separated, are you willing to be reconciled and restored to your spouse?
7. What scriptures can the two of you use to defeat a Dragon of Divorce?

Notes

CHAPTER 21

Do Marriage Dragons Have Any Good in Them?

*"The Lord is near to the brokenhearted and saves
those who are crushed in spirit." (Psalm 34:18)*

As one looks at each dragon represented in this book, one can see a lot of devastation and destruction that can happen if a dragon is released, not dealt with, and allowed to run rampant on a marriage.

There is a question of whether or not a marriage dragon has anything good in them. Thinking back to the beginning of this book, you can see I made a comment about how either a dragon is killed or the townspeople befriend the dragon. Now, we do not actually want to befriend one of these beasts, but they can be used to move our marriage forward, and maturity can take place.

Please allow me to explain how you can use a marriage dragon to help your marriage. Once a dragon is recognized, it is imperative that the husband and wife go into battle together. If the dragon is not slain but tamed, the marriage can also grow, and the dragon can be used to drive the marriage forward and be stronger.

Anytime there is a problem in marriage, the opportunity to grow will be there also. How you handle the dragon will depend on how much your marriage grows or stays stagnant in the problem. Dragons give you the opportunity to have a stronger marriage and prepare you for the next dragon that shows up.

Your marriage will be tested. Satan wants your marriage to fail, and he will not stop attacking. As he sends his dragons into your marriage, he waits and hopes that you will fail. When a husband and wife put on their battle gear and fight the dragon together, something wonderful happens. As Satan wants to divide couples, he will be frustrated when the husband and wife work together.

Look at Ecclesiastes 4:9–12 again. When two come alongside with God, that trio becomes a force that Satan will run from. Satan can make life a little difficult, but God will use that difficulty to strengthen the marriage and, more importantly, will make that couple stronger in their faith.

My question to you is this: "Are you broken? Are you crushed in spirit? Do you believe that there is no hope for your marriage?" I have good news for you: there is always hope. It may look like your marriage is over and that there is no light at the end of the tunnel. However, all dragons can be defeated, and the lessons learned from that particular dragon can be used to have a marriage that others will look at and desire the same strong marriage.

Jesus tells us in Matthew 5:13–16 how we should appear to the world: "You are the salt of the earth; but if the salt has become tasteless, how can it be made salty again? It is no longer good for anything, except to be thrown out and trampled under foot by men. You are the light of the world. A city set on a hill cannot be hidden; nor does anyone light a lamp and put it under a basket, but on the lampstand, and it gives light to all who are in the house. Let your light shine before men in such a way that they may see your good works, and glorify your Father who is in heaven."

What a wonderful testimony to the world when we glorify God and come through some trials in our marriages! God has never told us that we will have it easy, but He has said that we can do things through His strength and not ours. Matthew 11:28–30 says, "Come to Me, all who are weary and heavy-laden, and I will give you rest. Take My yoke upon you and learn from Me, for I am gentle and humble in heart, and you will find rest for your souls. For My yoke is easy and My burden is light."

You may be weary, tired, and ready to give up. Lean on God, and hang on to Him and His Word, and He will get you through.

Learn from your dragons, and allow them to help you move closer to God and your spouse. Dragons are inevitable, and every married couple will have to fight a few of them during their lives together.

Discussion Questions for the Good in Marriage Dragons

1. How do you view your marriage dragons? Do you learn from them or let them take something away from you that could have been a valuable lesson?

2. Have you grown from battling and slaying a marriage dragon?

3. If you are battling a marriage dragon, do you see God in the midst of the battle? Are you looking for Him, and what He is doing to help you?

4. Are you weary from your marriage dragon? What are some of the ways you can regain your strength?

5. What scriptures can the two of you use to understand the good in Marriage Dragons?

Notes

CHAPTER 22

Conclusion

"The Lord shall cause your enemies who rise up against you to be defeated before you; they will come out against you one way and will flee before you seven ways." (Deuteronomy 28:7)

Though the passage of Scripture above was not written directly to us, it was written *for* us and can be applied to our lives today for encouragement. There are enemies that are against your marriage and will do whatever they can to make sure that your marriage is damaged or destroyed. It is up to us to make sure that the dragons that come into our lives do little to no damage.

When we recognize a marriage dragon, we are called to act to defend against and defeat that particular dragon. It is important that we realize that we are in a spiritual battle against these beasts and that with Jesus Christ as our savior, we can defeat them. Ephesians 6:12 says, "For our struggle is not against flesh and blood, but against the rulers, against the powers, against the world forces of this darkness, against the spiritual forces of wickedness in the heavenly places."

Those circumstances that come against you are from Satan, who releases his dragons into your lives and marriages. He hates you, and he hates God, and nothing would please him more than to see your marriage, family, and relationship with God destroyed.

We must keep in mind that God is in complete control of the situation. Satan can do no more than God allows to us in our lives. If you need biblical proof, read Job 1 and 2, and you will see exactly how Satan works. It is all under the watchful eye of God. God has him on a leash and will pull him back when it is the time to do so.

However, as we have a will of our own, there may be a time when we listen to Satan's voice and follow him instead of the Good Shepherd, and that is where we get into trouble. By listening to the wrong voice, we will make decisions that release a dragon into our marriage, but remember, while we are struggling through the battle, God is always there. He has promised to never leave us or forsake us in Deuteronomy 31:6.

Scripture tells us that God will go ahead of us. I do not know about you, but I want God to be in front of me making a way, especially when that path looks hopeless. With God in front of us, we can be victorious, and more importantly, God will be glorified in that victory.

One of the best ways to defeat a marriage dragon is to pray together with your spouse each and every day. By doing this, you are keeping God in the midst of your struggle, and He will show you, through the power of His Holy Spirit, the best way to defeat your dragon.

Some of you may not be praying with your husband or wife every day, and you may not know how to go about starting this time of prayer. Let me give you some help with this. The first thing you should do is figure out a time that works best for you. That may be morning or evening. Misty and I pray together right before we go to sleep. It is what works best for us, and we can go to sleep with prayers on our hearts and minds.

If you have children, you may have to adjust your time after they are in bed. I have heard from couples with children say that they just do not have the time to pray because of their children. My response to that statement is that eventually they have to go to sleep, and when they do, they can pray.

Now I understand that there can be an exception when one of the children gets sick. I know this, but if you can get a time when they are asleep and make that time a habit, you will be well on your way to making sure you can have a daily prayer time. I can tell you that every single couple who has taken the "prayer challenge" from me has been successful.

My prayer challenge is this: pray together for thirty days, and see how your marriage strengthens. I can guarantee 100 percent that this time of daily prayer will strengthen and change your marriage. There is no way that it will fail. The daily prayer time for those who have taken this challenge has changed their marriage and made it stronger.

Does this mean that you will never have a trial? No, it does not. What it does mean is that when a marriage dragon attacks you, you will be better prepared for battle as a couple. If you add a daily devotion into the daily prayer time, now you have God's Word that will strengthen you further.

Some of you might be saying to yourself that prayer is a personal thing between you and God and you would rather not pray together with your spouse. This is dangerous thinking, and it is exactly what Satan wants you to believe. Now it is true that you should have personal prayer time, but I can also tell you that almost every single woman I have ever spoken to, in any marriage group I was leading, has told me that they wish that their husbands would pray with them daily. That tells me that husbands are failing their wives as a spiritual leader of their homes.

Yes, husbands, it is your responsibility to lead your wives and family. Ephesians 5:23 says, "For the husband is the head of the wife, as Christ also is the head of the Church, He himself being the savior of the body." Gentlemen, if you are submitting yourself to Christ, you will want to pray with your wives each day.

This time of prayer is so important, as without this time of prayer and devotion husbands and wives would not make it through some very difficult times in their marriages. Relying on God changes everything. Period. Marriage dragons are everywhere today, and they are looking for those marriages that may be struggling already. They are ready to attack and ravage your marriage and your lives. Please stay alert, and be ready to go into battle together.

Discussion Questions for the Conclusion

1. Husbands, are you having devotions, along with a time of prayer, with your wife every day? If not, why not?
2. Wives, are you allowing your husband to lead your home? If not, why not?
3. Wives, have you spoken with your husband about praying with you each day?
4. Husbands, if your wife has come to you asking you to pray with her, are you willing to take the lead and start a time of prayer today?
5. Husbands, are you willing to take the thirty-day prayer challenge with your wife?

Notes

Epilogue

God's Desire for You Reading This Book

"This is good and acceptable in the sight of God our Savior, who desires all men to be saved and to come to the knowledge of the truth." (1 Timothy 2:3–4)

Some of you reading this book are wondering how you can ask God to help you in defeating your marriage dragons. This may be something very foreign to you, or maybe even a little frightening. Let me tell you that nothing in this life is better than having a relationship with God through Jesus Christ. God wants our hearts. He wants us to love Him freely and to give our lives to Him. He wants us to receive the sacrifice of the free gift of salvation and spend eternity with Him.

This is nothing to be afraid of as He sent His only Son to die for all of us, which includes you reading this book. How wonderful is it that God loves you so much that He would also allow you to live *without* Him. He has given us the freedom to choose.

Every one of us is a sinner. Romans 3:23 says, "For all have sinned and fall short of the glory of God." All means all. Each and every person who has ever lived, is living, or will ever live. If you are reading this book, you are a sinner. Some of you have accepted the free gift of salvation, and some of you have not.

You may be thinking that if you accept this free gift that you will never have any fun or that your life will be boring. Nothing could be further from the truth. I began my personal relationship with Jesus Christ when I was almost thirty-five years old. I had lived a life that was riddled with sin, and as one who has lived with and without Jesus Christ, I can tell you that living with Him is better than without. Our definition of fun can be based on the world, and I can tell you that some of that "fun" is nothing more than sin and future pain camouflaged as fun. It will eventually lead you to an eternal place apart from a Holy God.

You may never have ever had anyone tell you this before, or maybe you have heard it and it did not make much sense. The reason for this confusion is found in 2 Corinthians 4:4: "In whose case the god of this world (Satan) has blinded the minds of the unbelieving so that they might not see the light of the gospel of the glory of Christ, who is the image of God."

In simpler terms, Satan has blinded many to the message of Jesus Christ and His free gift of salvation. If this is confusing to you, please pray that God will open your mind to what this is, and ask Him to show you Who He is. He will gladly do so.

If you are ready to have this relationship, all you need to do is follow a few simple steps:

1. Tell God that you are ready to receive His gift of salvation by forgiving you of your sins.
2. Recognize that you are a sinner, and tell God that you understand that you are a sinner and you need to be forgiven. Ask Him to forgive you of all your sins.
3. Receive His forgiveness through the shed blood of Jesus Christ on the cross.

4. Thank Him for this free gift of salvation.
5. Find a church that teaches the Bible, start attending, and begin to serve Him.

Some of you may think that God could never forgive what you have done. This is another lie from Satan. God is more than willing to forgive you for any sin that you may have committed, no matter how bad you think it is.

Give God a chance to transform your heart and show you how wonderful of a Heavenly Father He is. All you need to do is ask. The verse in 1 John 1:9 says, "If we confess our sins, He is faithful and righteous to forgive us our sins and to cleanse us from all unrighteousness."

God is faithful, and He is righteous, and He will forgive you. Please give Him the chance to show you how much of a loving Father He can be. Just sit and talk to Him right now, and receive the free gift of salvation.

ABOUT THE AUTHOR

Russell J. Lamendola was called by God into the pastorate many years ago and has a heart for teaching and preaching. He has a desire to see people grow in their relationships with Jesus Christ and to see others come to know that Jesus Christ is the only One who can cleanse people of their sin, change hearts, change lives, and strengthen marriages.

He received a bachelor of science in biblical studies in 2013 from Moody Bible Institute and a master of divinity in pastoral studies from Liberty Theological Baptist Seminary in 2016.

Russell has been married to Misty for over sixteen years. Shortly into their marriage, they both began to realize that marriage ministries were almost nonexistent, and this was a ministry that was desperately needed.

Eventually, God entrusted them to lead a marriage group. This group would help those who were struggling in their marriages and for those who just wanted a stronger, more biblical marriage.

This marriage ministry has continued for over a decade. During this time, they have seen marriages grow stronger through giving biblical teachings, sharing personal experiences, and having yearly marriage retreats.

CPSIA information can be obtained
at www.ICGtesting.com
Printed in the USA
BVOW08s1102260317
479476BV00001B/97/P